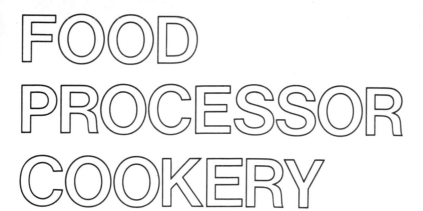

FOOD PROCESSOR COOKERY

Step-by-Step Guide to Success

Over 200 Easy Recipes

Margaret Deeds Murphy

Consultant: Rochelle Narotsky, Home Economist, Hamilton Beach

Dorison House Publishers / Boston

ISBN: 916752-30-5
Library of Congress Catalog Number: 78-72950
Manufactured in the United States of America
Fifteenth Printing

About the Author

Margaret Deeds Murphy, author and Home Economist, was born in Stromsburg, Nebraska, received her Home Economics degree from the University of Nebraska in 1937, and has been cooking, testing, and writing about food ever since. She is the author of a number of cookbooks, has been associated with several national magazines, was head of the Recipe Test Kitchens at General Foods Corporation as well as having her own consulting practice in New York City. Maggie, as she is known to her friends, lives with her husband on Cape Cod where she operates a test kitchen for the development of recipes and does food writing. She has prepared food pages for *Gray's Sporting Journal* and writes a weekly food column for the *Cape Cod Oracle* of Orleans, Massachusetts.

Contents

about food processor cookery

Welcome to the revolutionary new way to prepare food in your kitchen. Truly a space-age appliance, your food processor will chop, grind, slice, shred, puree, and whip foods with a touch of the button. Free from the tedious and time-consuming food preparation jobs, you will enjoy experimenting with new and formerly hard-to-do recipes. You'll prepare old favorites more quickly and easily than ever before.

Your food processor may well become your best friend as you find that it's saving you money, time, and energy. It's so easy to make fresh mayonnaise and salad dressings and save the cost of mixes and bottled dressings. You can chop or grind meats as you need them, using less expensive cuts; crumb bread for stuffing, toppings, fillers, and season to suit your taste; make fresh appetizers, dips, and sandwich spreads; turn nuts into butters and pastes, to use plain or to mix with other ingredients; puree vegetables, fruits, and meats for baby foods and other special diets; and make soups and sauces.

Working efficiently and with a minimum amount of time, your food processor speeds up the process of preparing foods that need to be sliced, such as fruits, meats, vegetables, and hard sausages. It grates cheeses, nuts, vegetables, and coconut in seconds. Vegetables, fruits, cheese, and chocolate are shredded in no time. And it quickly prepares chopped and minced vegetables, fruits, cheese, and meats. You'll be amazed at the time it saves you!

Although it uses little electrical energy, your food processor saves you effort simply by taking over so many of the jobs you used to perform by hand. It kneads bread doughs effectively and quickly, cuts shortening and butter into flour for pastry dough, and grates, purees, and mashes wherever the need arises. With the drudgery gone, cooking is never tiring.

The recipes in this book are kitchen-tested and include both plain and fancy dishes. With your food processor on hand as a daily aid, you'll be able to make all the things you've always wanted to try, but didn't have the time or patience for.

For instance, try fish quenelles for an elegant dish that was once considered a big job because all that raw fish had to be pulverized by hand. Now, a few seconds in the food processor, and it's done! Or how about making orange marmalade, which was always a labor of love, as it takes hours to prepare the oranges by hand. With your new assistant, it's no labor at all—just love! Cranberry bread is a delicious treat, but cutting up cranberries is no fun. The food processor chops the cranberries in seconds.

Pastry, as good as has ever been made with a pastry blender, comes from the processor in a trice. For a filling, imagine grated fresh pineapple! Easy with the processor. While it only makes 1 large or 2 small loaves of bread at a mixing, it is done so quickly you can make several batches one after the other without even washing the work bowl in between, so as not to waste oven heat while baking.

Ambrosia made with freshly grated coconut is now a breeze. And don't forget crepes, biscuits, muffins—all quick products from the processor. Not to mention almond paste, the basis for marzipan or those delicious almond macaroons. Leftovers become planovers with the processor. It truly is magic!

As with any new acquaintance, there is a period of getting to know each other. You'll find that there are some basic techniques to learn in order to get the best performance from your appliance. They are easily mastered by carefully reading the instructions that come with the machine and which are given in this book.

Remember, always, that the food processor is a powerful machine. When you are beginning to use it, particularly for chopping, check the size of particles of food after just a second. You can always chop longer, but can't put the food back together once it is too fine.

The food processor is a very unusual appliance. It is one of the few kitchen appliances that will actually become a part of you, as the results you get from it will begin to reflect your own cooking style. Technique is the key word in getting the full benefit from your food processor. You will find, as you become accustomed to working with your processor, you will develop a feel for each of the various tasks it is designed to perform. With experience, you will discover that your own food preparation and cooking techniques with your processor will become as familiar as paring an apple with your favorite paring knife.

Whether it's a cold Vichysoisse for a hot summer Sunday supper or a dinner party's grand finale of a dreamy Lemony Cottage Cheese Torte, you'll find cooking and dining more enjoyable than ever. So have fun with your food processor, and your friends and family will salute your new assistant.

using your food processor for best results

☐ Your food processor should be kept on your counter so that it is ready to use whenever you need it.

☐ Before putting a blade or disc in position, be sure to position the bowl and lock onto the base. Be sure the blade or disc is in place securely.

☐ Never remove cover before the blade or disc has stopped turning.

☐ Do not overfill the bowl. It will hold up to 4 cups of liquid ingredients or 6 cups of food that has been grated or sliced.

☐ Dry or solid ingredients should be processed before moist ingredients. Cut food into 1'' pieces before processing.

☐ Always turn motor off and unplug the machine before removing a piece of food that has become wedged between the blade and the side of the bowl, or if action stops during processing, or ingredients stick to the sides of the bowl.

☐ Do not overprocess food. Your food processor works in seconds, not in minutes, so large quantities can be processed in a short time. To process large quantities, divide the ingredients into small batches, and combine after processing.

☐ The type of food, and the process being used, will determine how much to put into tho bowl.

☐ Do not try to crush ice. This may damage the **steel blade**.

☐ Chop only one kind of vegetable at a time to get the most even results. However, you may chop a few together when the vegetables are to be pureed.

☐ To get perfectly even slices, pack the food chute tightly, so the food can't fall over sideways. To slice smaller amounts, such as a carrot, cut it up in pieces, or use the method shown on page 25. Before placing food in the chute, cut a slice off the end so that it rests flat on the disc.

☐ Never force food through the discs. Use moderate pressure for harder foods, such as carrots and cheese, and lighter pressure for more delicate foods, such as strawberries or bananas.

☐ More pressure will produce thicker slices; less pressure makes thinner slices.

☐ To help you in selecting vegetables and fruits that are just the right size to fit the chute, make a pattern on a piece of cardboard by drawing an outline of the top and bottom openings, and take it with you when you shop.

☐ A fork, long skewer, or toaster tongs is very useful to help position foods such as mushrooms, strawberries, or olives.

☐ To puree cooked fruits, vegetables, and meat for baby food or special diets, use the **steel blade**. For a smoother consistency, add some water, fruit juice, broth, or cooking liquid.

☐ Save time and energy by processing a large amount of baby food and freezing in portions.

☐ Pureed vegetables may be used to thicken soups and gravies. They thicken the liquid, give a richer taste, and cut calories since flour need not be added.

☐ A small piece of food may occasionally be left on top of the disc. This happens because of the space between the end of the chute and the top of the disc, and cannot be avoided.

☐ Chill foods before slicing and shredding for best results.

☐ Wider foods such as cucumbers, potatoes, or onions may be inserted through the bottom of the chute which is slightly larger than the top. Hold the food in place, then position the cover. This gives you larger, rounder slices with less trimming in order to fit the chute.

☐ Vegetables with high water content produce a lot of liquid when shredded or chopped. Drain this water off before using the food in a recipe.

☐ To prevent fruit from darkening after being sliced or cut, coat it in a commercial ascorbic acid mixture or lemon juice. If the fruit is cooked immediately, this is not necessary.

☐ Never use more than 3 cups of flour in the bowl when mixing and kneading the bread. It will generally hold enough dough to make an average-size loaf of bread. The bowl will hold thick cake batters of up to 4 cups.

☐ Leave the cover slightly ajar when the food processor is not in use to avoid strain on the locking switch and to allow the bowl to thoroughly air out.

☐ **Be sure to read the directions for use and care that come with your food processor.**

Here are a few important reminders:

1. To protect against electrical hazards, do not immerse base or motor in water or other liquid.
2. Unplug your food processor when it is not in use.
3. Do not use outdoors.
4. Blades are sharp and should be handled by the center post. Discs should be held by the edges. Don't let them soak in a dishpan of soapy water as you can get cuts by feeling around under the water to find them.
5. Never put your hand or any utensils in the container while processing. Always use the food pusher to feed the food into the food chute.

know your blades and discs

Your food processor comes with two blades, the **steel blade** and the **plastic blade**, and two discs, the **shredder** and **slicer discs**. You will soon learn to use the blade or disc that gives you the results you want.

Shredder disc (left) *gives you finely grated cabbage. Use* **steel blade** (center) *for an evenly chopped texture. Use* **slicer disc** (right) *for longer strips.*

jobs your food processor can do

plastic blade

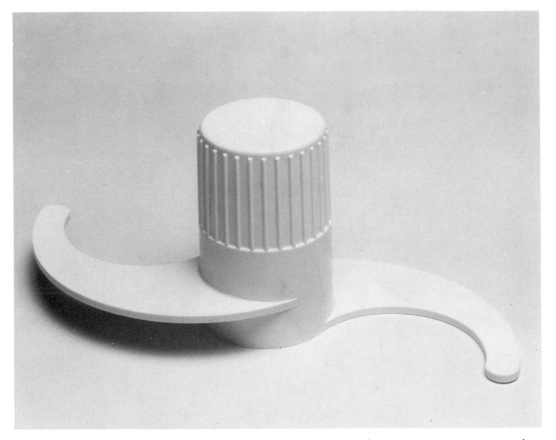

Use the **plastic blade** to mix or combine ingredients for sauces, soups, gravies, mayonnaise, dips, milk shakes, thin batters, and delicate foods. Place ingredients in the bowl and process to the desired consistency.

steel blade

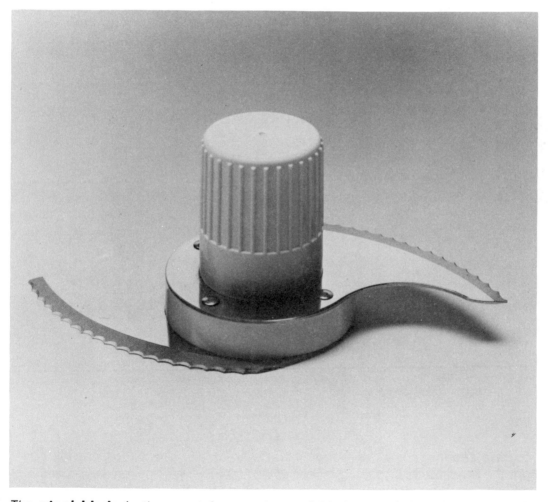

The **steel blade** is the most frequently used blade. It grinds, chops, kneads, blends, and purees. You can also use it to cut in shortening, mix and knead doughs, and mash fruits and vegetables.

*To **grate cheese**, cut the cheese into cubes and place about 6 or 7 in the bowl. With the **steel blade** in place, process using MOMENTARY on / off action until the texture is coarse (left) or fine (right), as you prefer.*

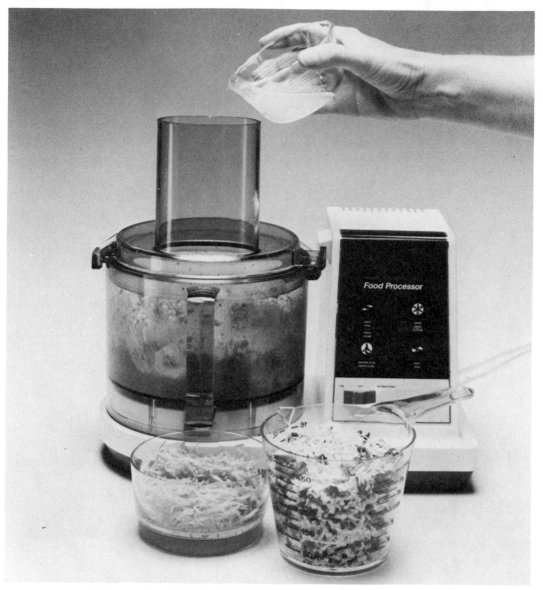

To **mix, cream, and blend** with the **steel blade**, you may add the ingredients through the chute. Nuts may be added whole to the mixture and they will be chopped satisfactorily. However, our recipes usually suggest chopping them beforehand. Thin pieces of orange and lemon peel may be chopped by adding them to the sugar-and-butter mixture rather than grating them by hand. Turn the machine off first and then push foods down from the sides with a rubber spatula.

To **chop meat**, cut meat into 1'' cubes, remove gristle and unwanted fat. Place 5 or 6 cubes into processor bowl with **steel blade** in place. Position cover with **food pusher** in chute. Process for 2 or 3 seconds for coarse texture (left); 3 to 4 seconds for medium (center); or longer for fine texture (right).

To **knead dough**, divide dough into 2 pieces. Break each of the pieces into 4 parts and press on the **steel blade**. Process until the pieces are combined into a ball. Break apart and repeat. Then repeat with the other half and combine the 2 kneaded pieces in a bowl. Allow it to rise.

To **make crumbs**, use the **steel blade**. Break up crackers, bread pieces, or cookies and place in bowl. Cover and process using MOMENTARY on/off action until you have the desired texture. The longer the processing, the finer the texture.

The bread shown in the picture has been processed a short time to achieve a coarse texture (left); only a few seconds more for the medium texture (center); and only a few seconds more for the fine texture (right).

To **puree nuts, vegetables, and fruit** use the **steel blade**. Peanuts, pecans, and other oily nuts can be pureed into a tasty butter easily and quickly. Dry-roasted nuts do not work as well because of the lack of oil. Process the desired amount of nuts to the coarse-chop stage, and add these coarsely-chopped nuts to the completed peanut butter to make crunchy nut butter. Use the **steel blade** to puree vegetables, fruits, and meats for baby foods, soups, sauces, and for diets which require soft foods.

Use the **shredder disc** to finely grate or shred cabbage, cheeses, chocolate, and nuts. You can also **julienne** vegetables and fruit with the **shredder disc**.

You can also **grate cheese** with the **shredder disc**. Place rectangular cut of cheese into chute. Press **food pusher** lightly for smaller pieces, harder for larger pieces.

To **make crumbs** with the **shredder disc**, place bread in chute as shown in the photograph and use the **food pusher** to press it against the disc.

The ***slicer disc*** *is used for making uniform slices of meats, cheese, poultry, fruits, and vegetables.*

slicer disc

To **slice vegetables, fruits, and cold meats** with the **slicer disc**, cut food into pieces to fit the chute and pack the chute tightly with food. Use **food pusher** to direct the food onto the disc. The lighter the pressure, the thinner the slices. The harder the pressure, the thicker the slices. Too much pressure may result in ragged and uneven slices.

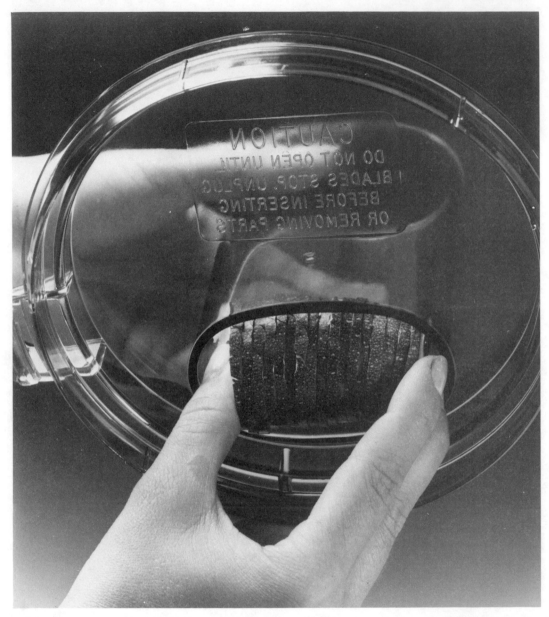

To make a true "matchstick" **julienne** cut of vegetables such as potatoes, summer squash, carrots, and beets, first place the food in the chute and slice. Remove the slices and reposition the **slicer disc**. Wedge a stack of slices vertically into the bottom of the chute, as shown in the picture. Slice again. These "twice-sliced" foods will then be square-edged julienne cut.

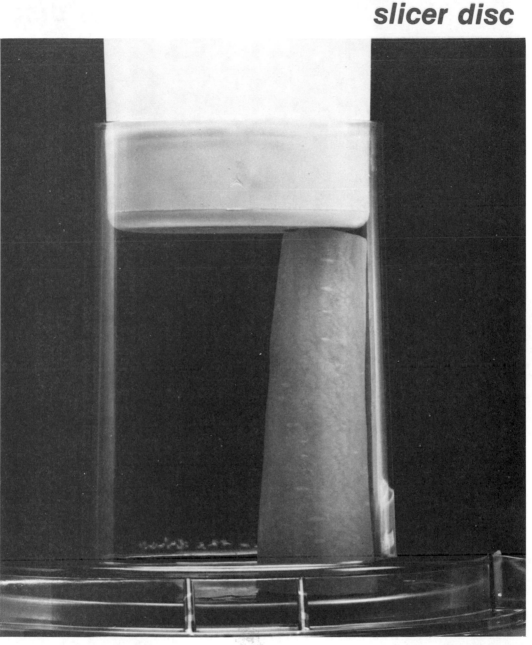

To **slice a single food**, place the food, like a carrot or a celery stalk, into the right side of the chute. Hold it firmly in place with the **food pusher**. The counter-clockwise rotation of the **slicer disc** will push the food against the right wall of the chute. This helps to hold the food upright for perfect slicing or shredding. Be sure the food is not tapered at the end.

To **slice small fruit**, choose fruit small enough to fit in the chute with little trimming. *Be sure they are firm, ripe, and chilled. Cut a thin slice off the end of the fruit before placing it in the chute so that there will be a smoother, flatter surface against the* **slicer disc**. *Use the* **food pusher** *to push the fruit through the chute. Peaches, apples, and other fruits of that approximate size may be cut into halves before putting them in the chute for slicing.*

To **slice strawberries**, hull firm, ripe, chilled fruit. Arrange strawberries on their sides for lengthwise slices, alternating their directions as shown in the photo so that they fit compactly in the chute. Slice using very light pressure.

To **slice chicken breasts**, first partially freeze boneless chicken breasts. Position them in the chute and from the bottom, filling the chute tightly. Slice using firm pressure.

Slices as shown here are perfect for stir-fry cooking.

To **slice sausages**, cut narrow sausages such as pepperoni or hard salami to fit the chute. Slice using firm pressure.

To **slice celery**, *cut crisped celery to fit chute. Pack so that the chute is full. Slice using firm pressure.*

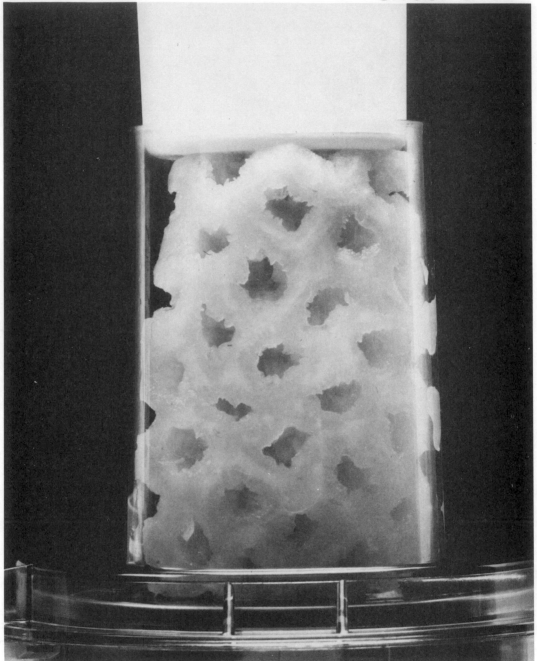

*To **slice pineapple**, peel and cut ripe, chilled fruit into wedges to fit chute. Use medium pressure to slice.*

To **slice radishes**, remove stem and root ends of radishes. Position in chute, closely packed. Slice using firm pressure.

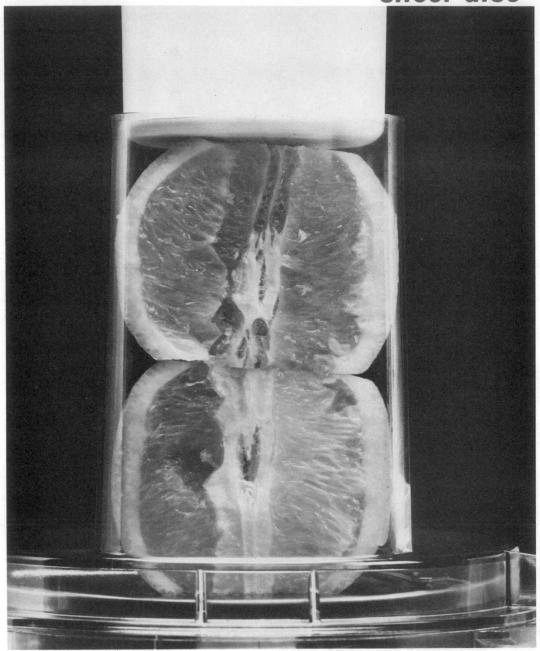

To **slice oranges**, *cut off ends of orange and cut orange in half lengthwise. Fit into chute from bottom. Use firm pressure to slice.*

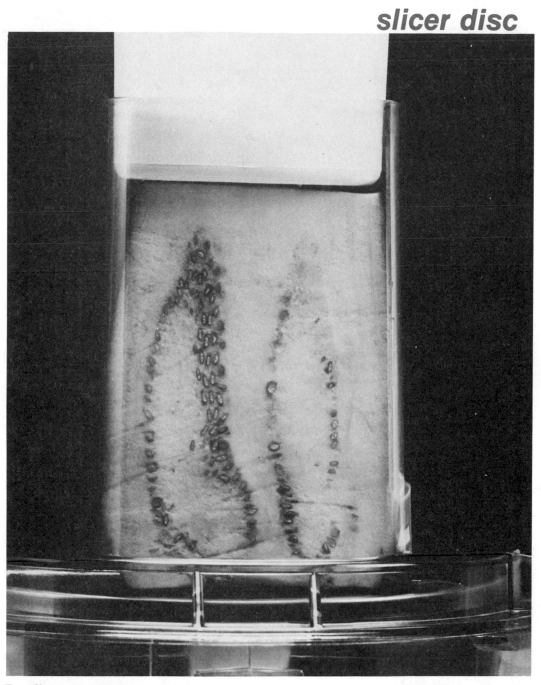

To **slice eggplant**, *cut peeled or unpeeled eggplant in pieces to fit chute. Use firm pressure to slice. Salt sliced eggplant lightly and let stand 5 to 10 minutes to remove moisture and prevent discoloration.*

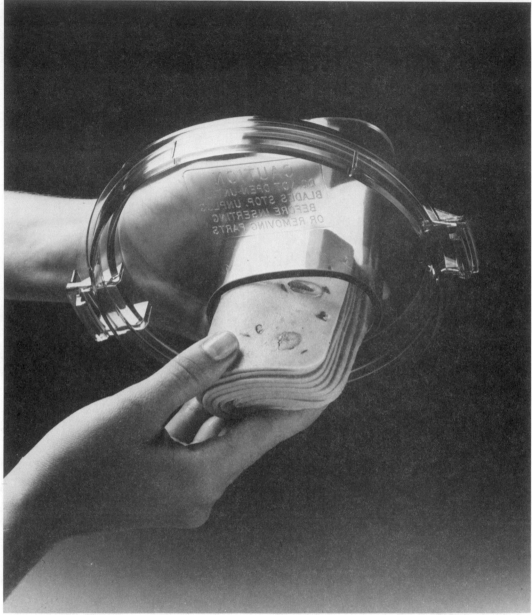

To **slice cold cuts**, *arrange several slices of chilled lunch meat—bologna, boiled ham, or other similar meat—into a stack. Fold and insert into bottom of food chute. Slice with firm pressure.*

French cutter disc

The **French cutter disc** was especially designed for foods which are deep-fat fried, foods which are to be dipped in batter, and foods which are to be pan fried. It can also thick-slice firm fruits like apples, pears, or pineapple for salads and snacks. Use it to make thick strips of ham and cheese for delicious chef's salads or appetizers.

To **French-cut foods**, place peeled or otherwise prepared food in chute and French-cut using firm pressure. The photo shows French-cut potatoes in the work bowl. In front, from left to right, cooked meat, cheese, and eggplant.

steel blade food processing yields

FOOD	AMOUNT	YIELD
Apple	1 medium, peeled, and cored.	½ cup.
Cabbage	¼ medium head cut into 1'' chunks.	¾ to 1 cup, short time coarse texture, longer time fine texture.
Carrot	1 medium, scraped, cut into 1'' pieces. Process 1 cup at a time.	½ cup.
Celery	2 firm ribs, strings can be removed if desired. Cut into short pieces.	½ to ¾ cup. Stop after 1 second, push down—process longer for fine texture.
Cheese	1½ ounces. Hard (Parmesan) cut into 1'' pieces. Process 6 to 7 cubes at a time.	¼ cup coarse or finely chopped.
Coconut	Fresh, 2 to 3 ounces, peeled, cut into chunks.	⅔ to 1 cup, short time coarse texture, longer time fine texture.
Cucumber	1 large, peeled. Cut in chunks.	1 cup, short time coarse texture, longer time fine texture.
Eggs	1 hard-cooked, chilled, and shelled. Dry well and quarter.	⅔ to ¾ cup. Coarse to fine texture.
Green Pepper	1 medium. Remove seeds and cut into 1'' pieces. Stop to push down.	¾ to 1 cup. Varies from coarse to minced depending on time.
Herbs	½ cup firmly packed.	⅓ cup finely chopped.
Leeks	1 or 2 medium, split and cut into 1'' pieces.	⅓ to ½ cup finely chopped for cooking.
Meat, uncooked	8 ounces chuck or other lean. Remove gristle, cut into 1'' cubes. Chop 5 to 6 cubes at a time.	1 cup; coarse, will have some larger pieces—fine will be even.
Meat, cooked (Beef, lamb, chicken, turkey, ham)	8 ounces, cut into 1'' pieces.	1 cup, coarse to fine or minced.
Mushrooms	3 large, 6 medium.	½ cup—good for pizza or other topping.
Nuts (Hard and soft)	1 cup.	1 cup finely chopped with some larger pieces.
Olives	10 extra-large stuffed.	⅔ cup, coarse to fine.
Onions	1 medium, quartered.	⅓ to ½ cup coarse to fine.
Pickles	3 large or 6 small. Cut into 1'' pieces.	⅔ to 1 cup; coarse to fine.
Potatoes	1 medium, quartered.	¾ cup; coarse to fine.
Shallots	5 to 6 whole, peeled.	¼ cup; coarse to fine.
Squash (Zucchini, yellow)	1 medium, cut into 1'' pieces.	1 to 1¼ cups—fine chop.
Squash (Acorn, Butternut)	½ of medium squash.	⅔ to 1 cup—coarse to fine.
Watercress	¼ cup, firmly packed.	¼ cup, fine.

For 1 Cup Crumbs Use	Number
Saltine squares	28
Graham cracker squares	22
Zwieback slices	7 to 9
Vanilla wafers	22 to 26
Chocolate wafers	16 to 18
Ginger snaps	16 to 18
Bread slices	2

shredder disc food processing yields

FOOD	AMOUNT	YIELD
Apple	1 medium (5 to 6 ounces) peeled or unpeeled cored; cut into halves or quarters.	1 cup.
Beets (Cooked or raw)	3 medium (2 ounces).	1½ cups.
Cabbage	¼ medium head, cut into sections to fit chute.	1½ to 2 cups.
Carrots	1 medium, cut into pieces. Arrange on sides in chute.	½ to ¾ cup.
Cheese, soft (Cheddar, Swiss, Mozzarella)	2-ounce pieces chilled.	½ cup.
Chocolate	1 1-ounce square, 1 4-ounce bar.	¼ cup, fine. 1 cup, fine.
Coconut	1 small coconut, peeled, cut into chunks.	2½ cups, coarse.
Cucumber	1 large, peeled. Remove seeds, cut into pieces.	1 to 1⅓ cups, coarse.
Green Pepper	1 medium, remove seeds and cut to fit chute.	¾ cup.
Mushrooms	3 large or 6 medium.	1 cup.
Nuts (Hard and soft)	½ cup.	½ cup.
Onions	1 medium, cut into quarters.	½ cup, coarse.
Potatoes	1 medium, cut into quarters—place in cold water to prevent darkening.	1 cup.
Squash (Zucchini, yellow)	1 medium, cut to fit chute.	1 cup.
Squash (Acorn, Butternut)	½ medium, cut to fit chute.	1 cup.
Sweet potatoes	1 small, peeled, and cut into pieces to fit chute.	¾ to 1 cup.

slicer disc food processing yields

FOOD	AMOUNT	YIELD
Apple	1 medium (5 to 6 ounces), peeled and cored.	½ to ¾ cup thin slices.
Banana	1 ripe firm, peeled.	1 cup thin slices.
Beets . . . . (Cooked or raw)	3 medium (2 ounces each).	2 cups even slices.
Broccoli stems . . .	2 or 3, trimmed.	1½ to 2 cups.
Cabbage	¼ medium head.	1½ to 2 cups.
Carrots	2 medium, cut in half.	1 cup or more.
Celery	2 firm ribs, strings removed.	½ to ¾ cup.
Cheese	4-ounce piece, cold.	⅔ cup—about 12 slices.
Cucumber	1 large, peeled.	1½ cups thin slices.
Eggplant	1 medium, peeled.	2 cups.
Green Beans	20 to 24 beans, placed on side.	2 cups, French cut.
Green Peppers . . .	1 medium, cut in half.	¾ cup half slices.
Leeks	2 medium, cut into pieces.	½ cup.
Lemons/Limes . . .	Small, trim thin piece off each end.	⅔ cup medium slices, 10 to 12
Lettuce	¼ firm head.	1 cup, sliced.
Meat, uncooked . .	8-ounce piece chuck (remove gristle), meat should be partially frozen for easier slicing.	¾ to 1 cup, uneven slices, good for oriental cooking.
Mushrooms	3 large, 6 medium, arranged on sides in chute,	½ to ¾ cup straight and diagonal slices.
Olives	10 extra-large stuffed.	⅔ cup sliced.
Onions	1 medium (3 to 4 ounces).	½ cup.
Pickles	3 large, 6 small.	1 cup.
Pineapple	1 medium, peeled, cored and quartered.	4 cups, thin slices.
Potatoes	1 medium.	¾ cup.
Salami	1 small, thin salami.	1 to 1¼ cups slices.
Squash . . . . (Zucchini, yellow)	1 medium.	1 cup, even slices.
Squash . . . . (Acorn, Butternut)	½ of medium squash.	1 to 1½ cups, medium slices.
Strawberries	6 medium, firm and hulled.	⅔ cup, even slices.

french cutter disc
food processing yields

FOOD	AMOUNT	YIELD
Apple	1 medium, peeled or unpeeled, halved or cored.	1 cup thick strips.
Cheese, Semi-soft (Cheddar, Swiss)	4 ounces, cut to fit width of chute.	About 1 cup thick julienne.
Cucumber	1 medium, peeled.	1 cup for salads.
Eggplant	1 medium, peeled or unpeeled.	3 cups for frying.
Ham, boiled	4-ounce chunk, cut to fit width of chute.	About 1 cup thick julienne.
Pear	1 firm ripe, halved, and cored.	1 cup thick strips.
Pineapple	1 medium, peeled, cored, and quartered.	4 cups thick strips.
Potato	1 medium, peeled, cut in half width-wise to fit chute.	1 cup French fry cuts.
Squash (Zucchini, yellow)	1 medium, cut in 2½''-wide pieces.	1 cup for frying.
Sweet Potato	1 medium, peeled, cut in half width-wise to fit chute.	1 cup French fry cuts.

how to adapt any recipe to the food processor

You can use your food processor to help you prepare your own favorite recipes. First, read through the recipe and note how it can be rearranged for the food processor to do the work.

It is usually easier to chop, slice, mince, grate, and crumb ingredients first, set them aside, and then continue with blending, creaming, mixing, and other combining instructions. Process dry ingredients such as nuts, crumbs, coconut, and similar foods first. Then other instructions can be followed, adding ingredients to the same processor bowl. But, if nuts are part of a cookie recipe, for example, they can be added whole (uncut) to the creaming process, where they will be cut up at the same time the shortening and sugar are creaming. You even have a choice!

As you use the food processor, you will realize that it often needs only a rinsing between "jobs" so that you can proceed from one to the other with ease.

Here is an example of how a recipe can be easily adapted:

nutsies

2½ cups whole wheat flour
2 teaspoons baking powder
¼ teaspoon salt
1 cup chopped almonds
½ cup shortening

1⅓ cups sugar
2 teaspoons vanilla extract
4 teaspoons grated orange rind
2 eggs
¼ cup milk

Mix flour, baking powder, and salt. Stir in nuts. Cream shortening and sugar until light and fluffy. Beat in vanilla, orange rind, and eggs. Add flour mixture alternately with milk, stirring just to blend. Spread in a greased and floured 15" x 10" shallow pan. Bake at 350°F for 18 to 20 minutes. While still warm, cut into squares. Cool.
Yield: 60 squares

To adapt this recipe to the food processor: Mix flour, baking powder, and salt in separate bowl. Cream shortening and sugar in food processor bowl until light and fluffy. Add whole nuts and several pieces of orange rind to creaming process. Add eggs, milk, and flour mixture to creamed mixture through chute all at once. Process just to blend. Spread in a greased and floured 15" x 10" shallow pan. Bake at 350°F for 18 to 20 minutes. While still warm, cut into squares. Cool.

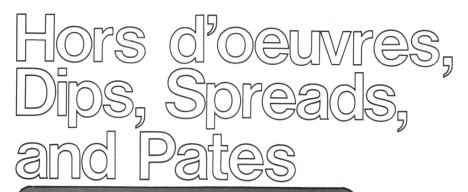

Hors d'oeuvres, Dips, Spreads, and Pates

Designed to whet the appetite by their taste and eye appeal, hors d'oeuvres, dips, spreads, and pates can range from the very simple to the extremely elaborate. Whichever way your taste runs, the food processor is there to help. If you wish to serve cucumber sandwiches, zap—and the food processor has thinly-sliced a whole cucumber. Or to prepare an elaborate pate—the "en croute" comes from the processor in a jiffy, as well as the pate, with its many ingredients, beautifully blended and ready to be baked.

Garnishes such as grated carrots, chopped parsley, and grated radishes are all ready with a minimum of fuss.

Follow our recipes or adapt your own to the food processor. Either way, you are in for pleasant preparation.

guacamole

Guacamole is of Mexican ancestry and it seems there are as many recipes as cooks. We give several variations on the basic avocado dip. The dip can be processed to be smooth, or leave pieces of avocado remaining in the mixture, as the Mexicans do. Its partner is corn chips.

1 clove garlic
1 teaspoon salt
1 tablespoon lime or lemon juice

Dash Tabasco sauce
¼ teaspoon Worcestershire sauce
2 ripe avocados

Lock bowl in position and insert **steel blade** inside. Add garlic and seasonings and process to chop garlic. Peel, remove seed, and cut avocados into pieces to fit chute. Add and process just to blend. Spoon into a serving dish. Cover by putting wax paper or plastic wrap directly on avocado. Chill.
Yield: About 1½ cups

Guacamole with Tomatoes: To the garlic and seasoning mixture add 1 small onion cut in pieces, ¼ cup dairy sour cream, 1 teaspoon chili powder. Process to blend. Add avocados and 2 ripe tomatoes, peeled and cut into pieces to go into chute. Process to blend. Cover and chill.
Yield: About 3 cups

Guacamole with Cottage Cheese: Omit garlic. Add ½ small onion and 1 cup cottage cheese to seasonings. Process to blend. Add avocados as directed and process to blend. Cover and chill.
Yield: About 3 cups

Avocado with Yogurt: Combine 1½ cups plain yogurt, ¾ teaspoon salt, 2 tablespoons chives, and 2 avocados, peeled and seeds removed, in processor with **steel blade**. Process just to blend. Cover and chill.
Yield: About 3 cups

seasoned butters

Seasoned butters are a delightful way to flavor party or family sandwiches. Most can be stored for a week in the refrigerator—ready at hand to use as desired. Soften the butter at room temperature and do not overprocess.

Anchovy Butter

4 anchovy fillets	**¼ teaspoon paprika**
2 teaspoons lemon juice	**1 cup (2 sticks) butter**

Lock bowl in position and insert **steel blade**. Add anchovy fillets, lemon juice, and paprika. Process on MOMENTARY until blended. Cut butter into pieces, add through chute, and process just to blend. Use anchovy butter as a spread for cucumber sandwiches, topping for broiled steak or fish, or on crackers.
Yield: About 1 cup

Cheese Butter

½ cup Roquefort cheese	**1 cup (2 sticks) butter**

Soften cheese and butter at room temperature. Cut butter into pieces. Lock bowl in position and insert **steel blade**. Add cheese and butter and process just to blend. Use cheese butter as a spread for meat and fish sandwiches, topping for broiled hamburgers, or on crackers. In place of Roquefort cheese one may use smoky-flavored soft cheese or pimiento cheese spread.
Yield: About 1½ cups

Herbed Butter

1 cup (2 sticks) butter	**1 3"-sprig fresh tarragon**
10 sprigs parsley	**Several sprigs fresh thyme**
3 or 4 large leaves fresh basil	**1 teaspoon lemon juice**

Soften butter at room temperature. Lock bowl in position and insert **steel blade**. Cut butter into pieces and add with herbs and lemon juice to bowl. Process just to blend. Herb butter can be used for sandwiches, spreading on broiled meat or fish, or on crackers. This combination is just one suggestion—you may have your own favorites. Dried herbs can be used in smaller quantities than fresh.
Yield: About 1 cup

steak tartare

With a processor you can now make steak tartare at home and regulate exactly the kind of beef that goes into its preparation. It is a sophisticated hors d'oeuvre rapidly gaining popularity.

10 sprigs parsley	**1 teaspoon salt**
1 medium onion	**½ teaspoon fresh ground pepper**
1 pound sirloin of beef without fat	**Sharp mustard**

Lock bowl in position and insert **steel blade.** Add parsley and process on MOMENTARY just until chopped. Remove to bowl, cover, and refrigerate. Cut onion into fourths and process until finely chopped. Remove to bowl. Cut meat into 1" cubes and process through chute 1 cup at a time until finely chopped. Remove after each processing to bowl with onion. When all meat is processed, add salt and pepper to meat and onion and mix well. Shape into 1" balls and roll in chopped parsley. Chill well. Serve with a small bowl of sharp mustard.

This is the simplest recipe for steak tartare. A more elaborate recipe might have 2 anchovy fillets processed with the onions and ¼ cup capers mixed into the beef after it is ground.
Yield: About 20 balls

swiss cheese and bacon spread

This is a tasty combination. It will store in the refrigerator for several days. Bring to room temperature and spread on thinly-sliced rye bread or crackers, or fill a decorative bowl and let guests do their own. This spread can be put on crackers and broiled to serve hot.

4 slices bacon	**¼ cup butter or margarine, softened**
5 ounces Swiss cheese	**¼ cup sharp mustard**

Fry bacon crisp. Lock bowl in position and insert **shredder disc**. Cut cheese to fit chute. Insert cheese in chute and grate. Remove **shredder disc** and insert **steel blade**. Break bacon into several pieces. Add with butter and mustard to cheese. Process to blend.
Yield: 1½ cups

basic cream cheese spread

Cream cheese makes a fine base for many spreads and dips. Always soften to room temperature for processing. This basic spread with many variations will be a constant helper when entertaining. Most cream cheese mixtures can be refrigerated for several days. Serve with celery, carrot sticks, and other raw vegetables.

1 package (8 ounces) cream cheese, softened
4 tablespoons mayonnaise

½ teaspoon salt
1 teaspoon prepared mustard

Cut cheese into several pieces. Lock bowl in position and insert **steel blade**. Add cheese and remaining ingredients. Process just to blend.
Yield: 1 to 1¼ cups

Onion Cream Cheese Spread: Process 2 green onions, tops and bottoms, and 6 sprigs parsley with **steel blade** before adding cream cheese and seasonings.
Yield: About 1 to 1¼ cups

Nut Cream Cheese Spread: Add ½ cup pecans or cashews through chute after ingredients are blended and process until nuts are chopped.
Yield: About 1 to 1½ cups

Egg Cream Cheese Spread: Add 1 tablespoon Worcestershire sauce and 1 small onion cut into fourths to process with cream cheese and seasonings. Add 2 hard-cooked eggs, peeled and cut to go through chute. Process on MOMENTARY until eggs are just blended.
Yield: About 1 to 1½ cups

Roquefort and Cream Cheese Spread: Add 1 tablespoon Worcestershire sauce, 1 small onion cut into fourths, and 4 ounces Roquefort cheese to cream cheese and seasonings and process to blend.
Yield: About 1 to 1½ cups

Shrimp Cream Cheese Spread: Add 1 can (4¼ ounces) shrimp, well drained, and 1 tablespoon lemon juice to basic cream cheese after cheese and seasonings are blended. Process to chop shrimp.
Yield: About 1 to 1½ cups

Tuna and Cream Cheese Spread: Add 1 can (6½ ounces) tuna fish, well drained, and 1 tablespoon lemon juice to basic cream cheese after cheese and seasonings are blended. Process to blend tuna.
Yield: About 1 to 1½ cups

pate en croute

For a glamorous hors d'oeuvre, nothing surpasses pate en croute. It's a double treat with a filling of savory chicken liver pate in a delicate crust—easier done than said with your food processor.

Pate

1 pound chicken livers	1 teaspoon fresh grated nutmeg
¼ cup butter	½ teaspoon ground sage
1 pound fresh pork with some fat	1 small onion, peeled, cut in quarters
1 pound veal	¼ cup brandy
3 teaspoons salt	½ cup dry white wine
Fresh ground pepper to taste	

Saute chicken livers in butter for 2 minutes. Cut pork and veal into 1" cubes. Sprinkle salt, nutmeg, and sage on cubes and mix meats and seasonings together. Lock bowl in position. Insert **steel blade**. Add meat cubes about a cup at a time and process until very fine. Remove to a bowl after each processing. Add onion, chicken livers, and butter in which they were cooked, and process until smooth. Gradually blend in brandy and wine. Mix with chopped meats. Add more wine if mixture seems too dry.

Crust

2 cups all-purpose flour	2 egg yolks
½ teaspoon salt	¼ cup cold water
½ cup chilled butter	

Lock bowl into position. Insert **steel blade**. Put flour and salt into bowl. Cut butter into pieces and add to flour. Process until mixture looks like cornmeal. Through chute add egg yolks and gradually add cold water, processing until ball forms around the blade. Wrap in plastic wrap. Chill 1 hour or longer before using.

If you have a pate mold with hinged sides, when pastry is ready, place the mold on a baking sheet and roll pastry and fit into mold. If you do not, use a buttered 5" x 9" loaf pan. Roll ¾ of pastry into a large oval 14" x 14" and fit into pate mold or loaf pan. Pastry, if well chilled, does not need a floured board. Cut pastry off so that there is about ½" hangover at top rim. Spoon pate onto crust. Roll remaining piece to fit top. Moisten edges and seal with a decorative border. Prick top with fork and make a hole in center of top to allow steam to escape. Brush top with slightly-beaten egg white.

Cut leftover pastry into small decorative leaves and/or flowers and arrange on top, sealing on with egg white. Bake at 425°F for 1 hour or until pastry is browned lightly. If the edge starts to get too brown, cover with aluminum foil.
Yield: 18 slices

chicken liver pate

Smoothly blended in the processor, this chicken liver pate will disappear quickly. Buy Melba-thin sliced bread and make your own Melba toast to serve with it.

1 small onion, peeled and quartered	¾ teaspoon salt
½ cup butter	Fresh ground black pepper to taste
1 pound chicken livers	2 tablespoons dry sherry wine
¼ cup heavy cream	Parsley

Lock bowl in position. Insert **steel blade**. Chop onion. Melt butter and add chopped onion and livers. Saute over medium heat until just cooked, about 5 minutes. Cool slightly and position **steel blade** in bowl. Add livers, cream, seasonings, and sherry. Process using MOMENTARY until blended. Pack into a china or ceramic bowl and cover and chill at least 4 hours. Garnish with parsley to serve.
Yield: About 2 cups

baked cheese mushrooms

*The **shredder disc** makes quick work of shredding the cheese for these elegant stuffed mushrooms. They may be prepared in advance and heated when you're ready to serve.*

36 large mushrooms	4 ounces sharp Cheddar cheese, cubed
1 medium onion, peeled, cut in quarters	½ teaspoon salt
4 tablespoons butter	Fresh ground pepper to taste

Wash mushrooms. Remove stems and cut off tough ends of stems. Lock bowl in position. Insert **steel blade** and process mushroom stems and onion until very fine. Saute in 2 tablespoons of butter for 2 to 5 minutes over medium heat. Meanwhile, insert **shredder disc** in bowl and add cheese through chute until all is grated. Combine mushroom stems and grated cheese. Add salt and pepper. Cool.

Saute mushroom caps lightly in remaining butter. Place stem side up on baking sheet and fill caps with cheese mixture. Bake at 400°F for 10 minutes. Serve hot.
Yield: 36

canapes

The food processor can make magic to decorate open-faced canapes for a party, so take full advantage of it.

1. Grate carrots or red radishes to use as a garnish. Sprinkle around the edge or in the center of open-faced sandwiches made from one of the cream cheese spreads.
2. Chop parsley for a pretty touch. Spread butter or mayonnaise around the outside edge of open-faced sandwiches and roll in chopped parsley.
3. Slice cucumbers to use as garnish or for cucumber sandwiches. For garnish, cut slice almost through and reverse halves on top of filling. For cucumber sandwiches, spread bread rounds with seasoned butter or basic cream cheese spread. Lay a slice of cucumber on filling. Serve plain or garnish center of cucumber with a little grated carrot or radish.
4. Slice red radishes or carrots to use as a garnish.

mushroom spread

*This tasty canape spread can keep for days in the refrigerator. Mushrooms and onions are quickly processed with the **steel blade**, and ready to mix with the rest of the ingredients.*

1 medium onion, peeled, cut in quarters
2 tablespoons butter or margarine
½ pound mushrooms
2 tablespoons lemon juice

1 teaspoon Worcestershire sauce
Salt and fresh ground pepper to taste
3 to 4 tablespoons mayonnaise
Parsley

Lock bowl in position. Insert **steel blade**. Process onion until very fine. Saute onion in butter until lightly browned. Wash mushrooms and cut off stem ends. Process with **steel blade** a cup at a time until finely chopped. Add to onions and cook over medium heat, stirring until any liquid is evaporated. Cool. Add lemon juice, Worcestershire sauce, salt, and pepper to taste. Add enough mayonnaise to make mixture hold together. Chill well. Garnish with parsley and serve with Melba toast.
Yield: About 1 cup

hot eggs anchovy

A strong-flavored appetizer. It can be made ahead of time, and heated to serve.

1 medium onion, peeled and
    quartered
2 tablespoons butter
6 anchovy fillets

3 sprigs parsley
6 hard-cooked eggs
Dash Tabasco sauce
1 teaspoon thick steak sauce

Lock bowl in position. Insert **steel blade**. Add onion and chop fine. Heat butter in skillet and saute onion until tender. With **steel blade** in place, process anchovy and parsley until smooth. Cut eggs to go through chute, add eggs and seasonings and process until just chopped. Scrape from bowl into cooked onion and reheat. Serve hot on Melba toast rounds.
Yield: 1½ cups

meat balls

Set a chafing dish full of these hot meat balls on your cocktail table and let your guests help themselves. They'll be eaten in almost as short a time as it took you to make them.

1 pound beef, cut in cubes
½ teaspoon poultry seasoning
1 teaspoon seasoned salt
Fresh ground pepper to taste
1 egg

¾ cup crushed corn flakes
Flour
2 to 4 tablespoons butter or margarine
Chili sauce

Lock bowl in position. Insert **steel blade**. Process meat a cup at a time until finely ground. Remove meat to bowl after each processing. When all meat is processed, mix with seasonings, egg, and corn flakes. Shape into about 2 dozen small balls and roll in flour. Heat butter in skillet and brown meat balls on all sides. Serve hot with chili sauce.
Yield: 24 meat balls

hot tuna bites

For instant hospitality, take advantage of ready-made biscuits. Your food processor chops the filling made from items usually found on your pantry shelf and in your refrigerator.

½ rib celery
2 to 3 scallions
½ cup diced sharp Cheddar cheese
1 can (6½ or 7 ounces) tuna, drained

3 tablespoons mayonnaise
2 cans refrigerated biscuits
1 egg white, slightly beaten

Lock bowl in position and insert **steel blade**. Process celery and scallions, both green and white parts, until chopped fine. Remove **steel blade** and insert **shredder disc**. Add cheese through chute to grate. Remove **shredder disc** and insert **steel blade**. Add tuna and mayonnaise and process on MOMENTARY until blended with vegetables and cheese. Scrape down sides with spatula, if necessary.

Pat or roll each biscuit into a thin oval. Put a spoonful of mixture on half of oval. Brush edge with egg white, fold other half of biscuit over filling, and seal by pressing with tines of fork. Make a tiny slit in top and brush with egg white. Place on greased baking sheet and bake at 425°F for 15 minutes or until nicely browned. Serve hot.

Yield: 20 portions

Soups

It is interesting to note that the soup served in most European countries is pureed—not filled with pieces of vegetables or meat as soups in this country are apt to be. European soups are usually made with a very strong stock base and they are flavorful.

It is easy to make smooth, creamy soups with the food processor, and once you're accustomed to making them yourself, it will be homemade soups for you.

The capacity of the bowl is up to 4 cups of liquid, so you may find it necessary to prepare soups in several batches.

cream of carrot soup

When you need a hot soup in a hurry, try this pretty and good cream of carrot.

2 cups milk
1 tablespoon flour
2 tablespoons butter
½ teaspoon salt

1 cup cubed raw carrots
2 scallions, cut in 1" pieces
3 sprigs parsley
Fresh ground pepper to taste

Lock bowl in position. Insert **steel blade**. Put 1 cup milk and remaining ingredients in bowl and process to blend. Add remaining cup milk while processing. Pour into saucepan and bring to a boil, stirring. Let simmer 2 to 3 minutes.
Yield: 2 servings

shrimp wine soup

Here is a soup that will do credit to the most elegant dinner party, or serve as a lunch with French bread and salad.

1 medium onion
1 rib celery
2 tablespoons butter or margarine
2 tablespoons flour
1 cup chicken broth

1 cup dry white wine
1 can (4½ ounces) tiny shrimp,
    undrained
Salt and fresh ground pepper to taste

Lock bowl in position. Insert **steel blade**. Peel onion and cut into quarters. Wash celery and cut into 1" pieces. Place onion and celery in bowl and process to chop fine. Heat butter in saucepan and saute onion and celery until tender but not browned. Cool. Add with remaining ingredients to bowl and process with **steel blade** until smooth. Return to saucepan and cook and stir until mixture boils and is thickened.
Yield: 3½ to 4 cups

fish chowder

This hearty soup makes a wonderful cold day luncheon dish. Use any mild-flavored white fish in season.

4 ounces salt pork, chilled
1 medium onion
2 medium potatoes
1 teaspoon salt
Fresh ground pepper to taste

1½ cups water
1 pound white fish
2 tablespoons flour
3 cups milk
2 tablespoons butter or margarine

Place bowl in position. Insert **steel blade**. Cut salt pork into 4 pieces and process until finely diced. Put in 2-quart saucepan and fry until crisp. Meanwhile, remove **steel blade** and insert **slicer disc**. Peel and slice onion and potatoes. Add to salt pork with salt, pepper, and water. Cover and simmer about 20 minutes or until potatoes are tender. Remove bone and skin from fish, if any, cut into 2″ pieces, and process with **steel blade** until chopped. Add to potatoes and simmer 10 minutes. Add flour and 2 cups milk to bowl and process to blend. Add to fish mixture with remaining milk and butter. Cook and stir until mixture comes to a boil and is thickened.
Yield: 4 to 5 servings

quick borscht

When the weather is hot, start the meal with refreshing cold borscht. When it's cold outside, serve it hot with a boiled potato in it.

1 can (16 ounces) beets
4 bouillon cubes
3 cups boiling water

¼ cup lemon juice
Salt and fresh ground pepper to taste
¾ cup dairy sour cream

Drain beets. Lock bowl in position. Insert **steel blade**. Add beets and bouillon cubes. Process 1 or 2 seconds to chop medium fine. Combine boiling water with bouillon cubes and beets in a saucepan. Simmer 10 minutes. Chill. Add lemon juice and salt and pepper to taste. Serve with sour cream.
Yield: About 4 cups

cream of mushroom soup

Watch for mushroom "specials" and use them for this delicious and lovely soup.

½ pound mushrooms
1 small onion, coarsely cut
2 tablespoons butter or margarine
1 cup milk or half-and-half
2 tablespoons flour

½ teaspoon salt
1/8 teaspoon white pepper
2 cups chicken broth
5 or 6 sprigs parsley

Wash mushrooms and trim off tough ends. Saute with onion in butter for 5 minutes in a 6-cup saucepan. Let cool for 5 minutes.

Lock bowl in position. Insert **steel blade**. Add mushroom-onion mixture, milk, flour, and seasonings. Process until smooth. Pour back into saucepan, add chicken broth, and cook and stir until mixture boils and is thickened. Rinse out work bowl, lock in position, and insert **steel blade**. Add parsley and process to chop. Serve soup sprinkled with parsley.

Yield: 4 cups

onion soup

For a cold winter day, nothing tastes better than onion soup. Make beef stock, or a combination of beef and chicken stock, and freeze to have ready for soups, particularly onion.

1 large red onion
3 tablespoons butter or margarine
2 ounces Parmesan cheese

3 cups beef stock
4 slices French bread

Peel onion and cut to fit chute. In this case, don't try to get onions to fit chute, as partial rings are better for soup. Lock bowl in place and insert **slicer disc**. Process onion to slice. Heat butter in a 6-cup saucepan. Add onion and cook, covered, over moderate heat for 10 minutes. While onion is cooking, insert **steel blade** and cut Parmesan cheese into small cubes. Process a few at a time to grate.

Add beef stock to onion and heat to boiling and hold just below boiling for 5 minutes.

To serve, ladle soup into oven-proof soup bowls. Place a slice of French bread (a day or two old is better) in the soup and sprinkle with grated cheese. Put under broiler until cheese is browned and bubbly.

Yield: 4 servings

vichysoisse

This chilled potato soup can be served by the cup for a first course, or by the bowl for a substantial lunch. It can be made a day in advance.

3 leeks
1 small onion
4 tablespoons butter or margarine
2 large potatoes

3 cups chicken broth
1 cup light cream
Salt and white pepper to taste
6 to 8 sprigs parsley

Wash leeks well and use only the white part. Cut to fit chute. Lock bowl in position and insert **slicer blade**. Load leeks through chute and slice. Slice onion. Heat butter in a 2-quart saucepan and add leeks and onions and simmer, covered, until tender, about 10 minutes. Do not let brown. Meanwhile, peel potatoes. Cut to fit chute and slice. Add to cooked leeks with 2 cups of chicken broth and simmer, covered, for 30 minutes. Cool. Lock bowl in position. Insert **steel blade**. Puree half of cooled potato mixture until smooth and repeat with other half. Combine with remaining chicken broth and cream. Season to taste. Chill well. When ready to serve, chop parsley in bowl with **steel blade** and sprinkle on each serving.

Chilled soup should be slightly thick. If it seems too thick for your taste, add a little additional cream and correct seasonings.
Yield: 6 cups

pink velvet soup

Making glamorous soups from scratch is fun, but now and then it's convenient to pull something together from cans. The following suggestions might spark your own imagination.

1 can (10½ ounces) old-fashioned
    condensed vegetable
    soup

1 can (10¾ ounces) condensed
    tomato soup
1 soup-can water

Lock bowl in position. Insert **steel blade**. Add vegetable soup and process until smooth. Add tomato soup and process until blended. Pour into saucepan and add water. Stir to blend and heat to boiling point.
Yield: 4 cups

Other suggested combinations: Chicken gumbo with cream of asparagus, chicken noodle with cream of celery, and clam chowder with chicken gumbo.

cream of chicken soup

Delicately flavored and nourishing, this soup may be served hot or chilled. If the chilled soup is too thick for your taste, dilute with a little chicken broth. This soup is also good for baby or the sick bay.

2 pounds chicken (backs, necks, or wings)
3 cups water
1 onion, cut up
1 carrot, peeled and cut up

1 rib celery, cut up
1 teaspoon salt
6 sprigs parsley
3 tablespoons flour
2 cups half-and-half

Wash chicken and combine with water, onion, carrot, celery, and salt. Simmer, covered, 30 to 40 minutes. Cool enough to handle chicken pieces. Pull off all edible meat. Discard skin. Lock bowl in position. Insert **steel blade**. Add chicken meat, vegetables from broth, and parsley. Process to puree. Through chute add flour and 1 cup half-and-half. Process 1 or 2 seconds. Combine with remaining half-and-half and 2 cups chicken broth. Cook and stir until mixture boils and is thickened. Correct seasoning. Serve hot or chilled.
Yield: 6 cups

cantaloupe frappe soup

Serve well chilled—even slightly frozen, if you wish—as a first course.

1 ripe cantaloupe
2 tablespoons honey
¼ cup dry sherry

2 tablespoons lemon juice
Fresh mint leaves

Cut cantaloupe in half and remove seeds. Cut halves into quarters, peel and cube fruit. Place bowl in position. Insert **steel blade**. Add half of cantaloupe cubes and process to puree. Empty into a bowl and add remaining cubes, honey, sherry, and lemon juice. Process to puree and mix well with cantaloupe in bowl. At this point, taste. You may want to add more honey or sherry, depending on the flavor of the cantaloupe. Chill well or freeze to frappe stage. Garnish with fresh mint leaves.
Yield: About 4 cups

celery soup

Use the outside green celery ribs to give this soup a pretty color.

4 large ribs celery
½ green pepper, seeded
2 green onions
1 cup chicken broth or beef
      bouillon

2 tablespoons flour
2 tablespoons soft butter or margarine
1 cup milk
1 teaspoon salt

Wash celery and cut into 1'' lengths. Cut green pepper and onion into pieces. Lock bowl in position. Insert **steel blade**. Add vegetables and process a few seconds until coarsely chopped. Combine with broth or bouillon in a 6-cup saucepan and simmer 20 minutes. With **plastic blade**, process flour, butter, milk, and salt to blend. Add to celery and cook until mixture boils and is thickened.
Yield: 1 quart

pureed vegetable soup

This soup is of European origin. It could be served as a first course or with a sandwich for lunch.

1 slice bacon, diced
1 small onion, cut up
1 carrot, peeled and cut up
2 cups diced fresh cabbage

1 large potato, peeled and halved
4 cups beef stock or chicken broth
Salt and fresh ground pepper to taste

Partially cook bacon in a saucepan. Add vegetables and 3 cups stock or broth. Simmer, covered, 30 to 40 minutes until vegetables are soft. Cool for 15 to 20 minutes.

      Lock bowl in position. Insert **steel blade**. Puree vegetables in several batches until smooth. Add remaining stock or broth and correct seasoning. Reheat soup.
Yield: 5 cups

homemade vegetable soup

For those of you who make your own vegetable soup, the food processor is a real boon.

*There are a few cautions. Process only one vegetable at a time. Use the **steel blade**, unless it is something you prefer to slice. Watch like a hawk to keep the vegetables from being chopped too finely. A quick on/off flip of the switch will give you control of the size. Cut each vegetable to go into the processor into pieces the same size so that they will chop evenly. There may be one or two pieces which will escape the **steel blade**, and you can catch those with a knife. Here is a recipe, if you don't already have a favorite.*

1 quart beef stock
1 cup cut-up, cooked meat
2 cups assorted cut-up vegetables
    (onion, celery, carrots, or
    other vegetables in season)

1 cup canned tomatoes
2 tablespoons uncooked rice
3 or 4 sprigs parsley
Salt and fresh ground pepper to taste

Heat stock and meat in a 2-quart saucepan. Add vegetables which have been processed with the **steel blade**, tomatoes, rice, and parsley. Process parsley with the **steel blade** until finely chopped before adding to soup. Taste and correct seasonings. Simmer for 15 to 20 minutes until the vegetables are tender.
Yield: 4 to 6 servings

Main Dishes

Once you have made a few recipes specifically designed for the food processor, you will quickly learn how to adapt your own favorite recipes so that the processor does all the tedious chipping and chopping. The only caution—one more time—is to use almost an on/off motion of the switch when using the **steel blade**, so that you can control the fineness of the material. The incredible speed of the chopping makes it easy to get away from you.

beef in port wine

Serve over hot buttered noodles for a delicious dish.

2 pounds boneless beef chuck
2 medium onions
1 medium carrot, peeled
2 ribs celery
½ pound mushrooms
4 tablespoons butter or margarine

2½ cups boiling water
2 bouillon cubes
⅔ cup tawny port wine
½ teaspoon leaf thyme, rubbed
Salt and fresh ground pepper to taste

Freeze beef until firm but *not* frozen hard. Peel onions and cut to fit chute. Cut carrot to fit chute. Clean celery and cut to fit chute. Cut off tough stem ends of mushrooms.

Lock bowl in position. Insert **slicer disc**. Slice beef and vegetables. Heat butter in a large saucepan and as work bowl becomes filled, transfer food to hot butter and cook and stir until meat and vegetables are lightly browned. Add remaining ingredients and simmer about 2 hours or until tender. Toward the end of the cooking time, remove 1 cup liquid and cool. Lock bowl in position and insert **plastic blade**. Combine the 1 cup liquid with 4 tablespoons flour and process until smooth. Return to saucepan and cook until slightly thickened. Serve over hot buttered noodles.

Yield: 6 servings

Note: This recipe is also very good for venison.

beef and mushrooms

This is a tasty way to serve chuck beef.

2 medium onions
1 clove garlic
6 medium mushrooms
1 pound semi-frozen beef chuck
2 tablespoons cooking oil

1 teaspoon salt
1 tablespoon thick steak sauce
1 cup water
1 tablespoon flour
Hot cooked noodles

Peel onions and cut to fit chute. Peel garlic. Cut tough ends from mushrooms. Cut beef to fit chute. Lock bowl in position. Insert **slicer disc**. Process onions, garlic, mushrooms, and steak to slice, removing from work bowl as it becomes full. Heat oil in skillet and add onions, garlic, mushrooms, and steak. Cook and stir over high heat until lightly browned. Remove **slicer disc** and insert **plastic blade**. Add salt, steak sauce, water, and flour and blend for a few seconds. Pour over steak in skillet. Bring to a boil, reduce heat, cover, and cook about 1 hour or until tender. Serve with hot cooked noodles.
Yield: 4 servings

inside-out hamburger

Instead of putting the crumbs in the chopped beef, try putting them on the outside. With the processor the crumbs can be flavored any way you want.

4 slices white bread
1 clove garlic
2 pounds lean beef
2 tablespoons water

1½ teaspoons salt
Fresh ground pepper to taste
4 tablespoons butter or margarine

Place bowl in position. Insert **steel blade**. Break bread slices into pieces and put into bowl with garlic clove. Process until bread is in fine crumbs. Remove from bowl to a pie plate or wax paper. Cut beef into 1'' cubes. Sprinkle with water, salt, and pepper. Process 1 cup at a time until chopped medium coarse. Remove beef after each processing. When all beef is processed, shape into 6 patties. Press crumbs into all sides of patties. Heat butter in skillet large enough to hold all patties. Pan fry over medium heat about 6 minutes, turning to brown both sides for medium.
Yield: 6 servings

easy chinese chicken

*Easy Chinese chicken is just that, making no pretense of being a "real" Chinese dish. It's easy to prepare the chicken for stir-fry with the **slicer disc**.*

1 whole chicken breast
1 large onion
1 clove garlic
3 tablespoons oil

1 can (16 ounces) mixed Chinese
    vegetables, drained
2 tablespoons soy sauce
1 tablespoon cornstarch
½ cup chicken broth

Remove bones and skin from chicken breast. Wrap meat lightly in plastic wrap and place in freezer for about 1 hour. Combine bones and skin with a cup of water and simmer for 30 minutes. Reserve ½ cup broth.

Lock bowl in position and insert **slicer disc**. Cut onion to fit chute and slice. Slice garlic. Cut partially frozen chicken to fit chute and slice.

Heat oil in a large skillet or wok and quickly saute chicken, onion, and garlic, about 1 to 2 minutes. Push to one side and add drained vegetables. Heat until hot, another 2 minutes. Mix remaining ingredients. Stir chicken and vegetables together and add broth mixture. Bring to a boil. Serve at once with hot rice.
Yield: 2 to 3 servings

chicken hash

This dish, perfect for a light lunch or supper, can be prepared in advance, refrigerated, and heated when ready to eat. Add 10 minutes to cooking time if this is done.

2 ounces Parmesan cheese
1 small piece onion
1 rib celery, washed
3 cups cooked chicken pieces
2 tablespoons butter or margarine

1 can (10½ ounces) condensed cream
    of chicken soup
½ cup light cream or milk
2 eggs
¼ cup dry sherry

Lock bowl in position. Insert **steel blade**. Cut Parmesan cheese into cubes and process 6 to 8 cubes at a time until finely chopped. Remove from bowl. Cut onion and celery into 1" pieces and process until finely chopped. Cut chicken into 2" to 3" pieces and process until coarsely chopped. Heat butter and soup together. Add onion, celery, and chicken. Process cream, eggs, and sherry until blended and add to chicken mixture, stirring to blend. Spoon into a flat, 6-cup casserole. Sprinkle with Parmesan cheese. Bake at 400°F for 20 to 25 minutes, until hot and bubbly.
Yield: 4 to 6 servings

chickenburgers

The long-gone, famed Stork Club of New York City was renowned for chicken-burgers. Making them at home was a task reserved for the most special occasions. Now the food processor chops the chicken with ease, and the rest is done in a matter of minutes. No need to wait for a grand occasion to prepare them. Serve them on a bun, as a main course, or make tiny patties to fry and serve as hors d'oeuvres.

1 3-to-4 pound chicken	**Fresh ground pepper**
3 slices soft bread	**1 egg**
1 medium onion, cut in pieces	**Flour**
1 teaspoon salt	**Butter or margarine**

Cut chicken meat from carcass. Do not use skin. Save carcass and skin to make chicken broth. Cut chicken meat into 1" to 2" pieces. There should be about 2½ cups.

Lock bowl in position. Insert **steel blade**. Add bread, onion, salt, pepper, and egg. Process until onion is chopped fine. Remove to a bowl. Add chicken about 1 cup at a time and process with **steel blade** until finely chopped. Continue until all chicken is processed, adding to bread mixture after each processing. Mix lightly to blend. Chill well. Shape into patties. Dip in flour. Heat butter in skillet and saute patties over moderate heat, about 10 minutes, turning to brown both sides. Serve with chili sauce, if desired.

This is the basic chickenburger recipe. Variations can be made as follows: Add to bread mixture while it is processing—6 to 8 sprigs of parsley; or ½ teaspoon fresh grated nutmeg; or ½ cup blanched almonds; or ½ teaspoon poultry seasoning.

Yield: About 6 patties; or to serve on buns, makes 8; or several dozen of cocktail size.

chicken breasts with rice and vegetables

This is a fine company dish since it bakes while you are doing other things and can be prepared in advance.

2 whole chicken breasts
4 pieces celery
½ pound fresh green beans
2 large onions
2 large carrots
1 cup uncooked long grain rice
3 cups chicken broth

1 cup dry white wine
1½ teaspoons salt
Fresh ground pepper to taste
1 teaspoon leaf rosemary, ground in mortar with pestle
2 tablespoons softened butter

Bone chicken breasts and cut each into 6 pieces. Refrigerate. Cover bones with water and simmer 15 to 20 minutes, adding seasonings as desired. Strain. If less than 3 cups, add water.

Wash and trim celery, green beans, and onion. Cut into 1'' pieces. Peel carrots and cut into 1'' pieces.

Lock bowl in position and insert **steel blade**. Process vegetables in 2 batches until medium fine. Mix with rice, chicken broth, wine, and seasonings and spoon into a large, buttered casserole. Place chicken breasts on top. Cover casserole (if it has no lid, use aluminum foil). Bake at 350°F for 1½ hours or until rice is fluffy and chicken tender. Uncover and spread butter on chicken breasts. Bake 10 to 15 minutes longer.
Yield: 4 to 6 servings

skillet liver with sour cream

This is a good dish for the electric skillet, where the temperature can be controlled.

1½ pounds sliced beef liver
4 tablespoons flour
4 tablespoons butter or margarine
1 teaspoon salt
Fresh ground pepper to taste

½ cup water
1 beef bouillon cube
5 medium potatoes, peeled
2 medium onions, peeled
1 cup dairy sour cream

Freeze liver slices until firm but *not hard*. Lock bowl in position and insert **slicer disc**. Cut liver to fit chute and slice. Sprinkle with flour and brown in hot butter in a large skillet. Put ½ teaspoon salt and pepper to taste over liver. Add water and bouillon cube. Cut potatoes to fit chute and slice. Cut onions to fit chute and slice. Spread potatoes and onions over liver and add remaining salt and pepper. Bring to a boil, reduce heat, and simmer, covered, until potatoes are tender, 40 to 45 minutes. Spread sour cream over potatoes and allow to heat through. Serve liver and potatoes with sour cream gravy.
Yield: 4 servings

linguini with green cheese

A meatless entree combining spinach and cheese to make a perfect sauce.

8 ounces Parmesan cheese
1 package (10 ounces) frozen,
    chopped spinach
1 container (8 ounces) Ricotta cheese

1 tablespoon lemon juice
8 ounces linguini
2 green onions, cut up

Cut Parmesan cheese into 1'' cubes. Lock bowl in position. Insert **steel blade.** Process Parmesan until finely chopped, 6 or 7 cubes at a time. Remove to bowl as processed. Cook spinach as directed on package. Drain well. Process spinach and Ricotta cheese until blended and smooth. Put into the top of a double boiler. Stir in Parmesan cheese and lemon juice and heat over hot water while linguini cooks. Cook linguini in boiling, salted water (6 cups water with 2 teaspoons salt) until tender, yet firm, about 8 minutes. Drain. Serve linguini with green cheese sauce, topped with chopped onions.
Yield: 4 servings

chili chuck steak

The spicy, hot tomato sauce gives the chuck steak a fine flavor.

2 pounds beef chuck steak
2 tablespoons cooking oil
2 medium onions, peeled
3 medium tomatoes
1 clove garlic, peeled
1 rib celery

1 teaspoon chili powder
¼ teaspoon cumin
1 small piece hot pepper, if desired
1 teaspoon salt
Fresh ground pepper to taste

Remove fat and bones from chuck steak and cut into 6 servings. Heat oil in large skillet and brown meat on both sides. While meat is browning, lock bowl in position. Insert **steel blade**. Cut onions into eighths. Remove stem ends and cut tomatoes into 4 pieces. Cut garlic into 2 pieces. Wash celery and cut into 1'' pieces. Add vegetables and seasonings. Process until coarsely chopped. Pour over meat in skillet. Simmer about 1½ to 2 hours or until meat is tender.
Yield: 4 to 6 servings

welsh rabbit

Here is a quick and filling supper dish.

8 ounces sharp Cheddar cheese
1 egg
1 teaspoon Worcestershire sauce
½ teaspoon salt
½ teaspoon dry mustard

1 tablespoon cornstarch
1½ cups hot milk
4 pieces toasted bread or English
    muffins

Lock bowl in position. Insert **shredder disc**. Cut cheese to fit chute and process to grate. Remove **shredder disc** and insert **plastic blade**, leaving cheese in bowl. Add egg, seasonings, and cornstarch, and process to blend. While still processing, add milk through chute. When blended, pour into a heavy saucepan and cook and stir over low heat until thickened. Serve over toast or English muffins.
Yield: 4 servings

crepes

A glamorous dessert or main dish, these lightly sweetened crepes are great favorites.

½ cup all-purpose flour	1 teaspoon sugar
1 egg	1 cup milk
1 egg yolk	2 tablespoons vegetable oil
1/8 teaspoon salt	Oil for frying

Lock bowl in position. Insert **plastic disc**. Combine all ingredients in work bowl and process until blended and smooth. Chill batter for 30 minutes. Brush a 6'' to 7'' crepe skillet with oil and heat over moderate heat. Pour about 2 tablespoons batter into skillet and tilt so batter covers bottom of skillet. Cook until lightly browned. It should take about 2 minutes. Turn and cook 1 minute longer. Remove from skillet and cool on cake rack. If crepes are not to be used at once, they can be wrapped in plastic wrap and stored in the refrigerator or in freezer wrap and frozen for 0°F storage.

If a crepe-making machine is used, follow manufacturer's instructions.
Yield: About 16

Chicken Filling for Crepes

2 ounces Parmesan cheese	1 cup chicken broth
12 medium, fresh mushrooms	½ cup light cream
3½ cups cooked chicken, cubed	2 egg yolks
¼ cup butter	Salt and fresh ground pepper to taste
¼ cup flour	

Lock bowl in position. Insert **steel blade**. Cut Parmesan cheese into cubes and process 6 to 8 cubes at a time until finely grated. Remove and reserve. Cut off tough stem ends of mushrooms and rinse. Process until finely chopped. Process chicken with **steel blade** until finely chopped. Reserve. Heat butter in saucepan and cook chopped mushrooms for 5 minutes. Add flour to mushrooms, stir in chicken broth and cook and stir until mixture boils and is thickened.

In processor, blend cream and egg yolks with **plastic blade**. Stir into mushroom-chicken broth mixture. Season to taste with salt and pepper. Reserve a third of the sauce and add chicken to remainder. Put several tablespoons of this filling down the center of the light side of each crepe and roll crepe around filling. Transfer to a flat, buttered casserole, seam side down. Continue until all crepes and filling are used. Spread reserved plain sauce over crepes and sprinkle with grated Parmesan cheese. Bake at 425°F for 15 minutes or until nicely browned.
Yield: 6 servings

shrimp and eggs, chinese style

Here is a light supper dish. Serve with mustard and duck sauce.

1 medium onion, peeled
1 can (4½ ounces) tiny shrimp,
    drained
1 cup bean sprouts, drained

1 tablespoon soy sauce
6 large eggs
2 to 3 tablespoons butter or
    margarine

Lock bowl in position. Insert **steel blade**. Cut onion into eighths and process until finely chopped. Remove **steel blade** and insert **plastic blade**. Add shrimp, bean sprouts, soy sauce, and eggs and process just to blend. Heat butter in a 10'' to 12'' skillet. Pour in egg mixture. Cook over moderate heat until brown and eggs are set. Roll and cut into 4 portions to serve.
Yield: 4 servings

fruited ham loaf

Serve ice-cold dairy sour cream mixed with grated horseradish as a sauce with this flavorful loaf.

1 pound ham
½ pound veal
½ pound fresh pork
½ green pepper
4 cups corn flakes
1 cup milk
2 eggs

6 tablespoons brown sugar
1 tablespoon prepared mustard
2 teaspoons butter or margarine
½ teaspoon salt
1 can (1 pound, 1 ounce) apricot
    halves, drained

Cut ham, veal, and pork into 1'' cubes. Lock bowl in position. Insert **steel blade**. Process meat 1 cup at a time until finely chopped. Put into a bowl after each processing.

    Remove seeds and white rib from pepper and cut into 1'' squares. Put into work bowl with corn flakes, milk, eggs, 3 tablespoons brown sugar, mustard, butter, and salt. Process until blended. Add to meat in bowl and mix lightly to blend. Line bottom of a greased 9'' x 9'' x 2'' baking pan with apricot halves, cut side up. Sprinkle with remaining 3 tablespoons brown sugar. Spread meat mixture over apricots. (If necessary, add a little more milk.) Bake at 350°F for 1 hour and 20 minutes. Invert on platter to serve.
Yield: 8 servings

deer sausage

Deer meat is inclined to be very lean. A better sausage is made with it if mixed with a little fresh pork, as this recipe indicates.

1 pound boneless fresh pork, ¼ of which should be fat
2 pounds boneless deer meat
¾ teaspoon salt

2½ teaspoons poultry seasoning
½ teaspoon dried leaf sage, rubbed
Fresh ground pepper to taste
2 tablespoons water

Cut pork, pork fat, and deer meat into 1'' cubes. Mix together and sprinkle with seasonings. Lock bowl in position. Insert **steel blade**. Process 1 cup at a time, sprinkling a little water through chute while processing each cup. As each cup is processed, remove to another bowl. This method of combining meats and seasonings should require less mixing after processing. It will keep several days under refrigeration or about 2 months at 0°F when freezer wrapped.
Yield: About 3 pounds of sausage

To cook sausage, form into flat patties and pan fry over moderate heat, turning, until nicely browned on both sides.
Yield: 9 to 12 servings

turkey stuffing

Again, the food processor takes the hard work out of a holiday chore.

½ pound bread, dried
1 large onion, peeled
3 ribs celery
1 cup packed fresh parsley
1½ teaspoons dried sage
½ teaspoon dried thyme leaves

½ teaspoon salt
Fresh ground pepper to taste
½ cup butter or margarine
1 egg
⅔ cup chicken broth

Lock bowl in position. Insert **steel blade**. Break 3 or 4 slices bread into bowl at a time and process to coarse crumbs. As processed, remove to large bowl. Cut onion into eighths. Wash celery and cut into 1'' pieces. Process vegetables until finely chopped. Heat butter in skillet and add vegetables and seasoning and cook over low heat, about 10 minutes. Add to bread crumbs and mix well. With **plastic blade**, combine egg and broth. Mix into bread crumbs. Use as a stuffing for turkey. Note that this recipe, halved, may be used for a roasting chicken, but use 1 small egg.
Yield: 7 to 8 cups

aioli sauce

Here is a mayonnaise-like sauce for those who love the flavor of garlic. Use for fish, cold meats, or vegetables.

5 garlic cloves, peeled	1 tablespoon lemon juice
3 egg yolks	1½ cups salad oil
½ teaspoon salt	

Lock bowl in position. Insert **steel blade**. Add garlic, egg yolks, salt, and lemon juice. Process until garlic is finely chopped and egg yolks well beaten. While still processing, add salad oil in a thin stream through chute. When all oil is added the sauce should have the consistency of mayonnaise.
Yield: 1½ cups

broiled fish and topper

This is a tasty topping for almost any fish fillet, but it is particularly good with blue-fish or mackerel.

1 small onion	1 slice whole wheat bread
1 medium ripe tomato	1½ to 2 pounds thin fish fillets
4 sprigs parsley	2 tablespoons lemon juice
2 tablespoons butter or margarine	Salt and fresh ground pepper to taste
¼ teaspoon leaf tarragon	

Peel onion and cut into fourths. Cut tomato into eighths. Lock bowl in position. Insert **steel blade**. Add onion, tomato, parsley, butter, tarragon, and whole wheat bread broken into pieces. Process until blended.

Place fillets on a buttered broiler pan or flat baking pan. Pour lemon juice over fish and sprinkle with salt and pepper. Broil fish 3'' from source of heat for 5 minutes. Spread with topping and broil 3 minutes longer or until topping is hot and bubbly.
Yield: 4 servings

lobster delhi

Curried lobster is a treat. If you prefer a lighter curry flavor, reduce curry powder. Serve with fluffy rice and apple chutney.

2 slices bread
4 tablespoons butter
1 small onion
½ green pepper
3 cups, approximately, lobster meat
2 tablespoons flour

1 tablespoon curry powder
1½ cups chicken broth
1 tablespoon lemon juice
1 tablespoon orange marmalade
Salt and fresh ground pepper to taste

Lock bowl in position. Insert **steel blade**. Break bread slices into several pieces and put into bowl with 2 tablespoons softened butter. Process a few seconds until fine crumbs are formed. Remove from bowl and reserve. Peel and cut onion into quarters. Remove seeds and cut pepper into 1'' pieces. Process until chopped fine. Heat remaining 2 tablespoons of butter in a saucepan. Add processed onion and green pepper and saute until tender but not browned.

Remove any spines from lobster and process with **steel blade** to bite-sized pieces. Use MOMENTARY to control size.

Add flour and curry powder to cooked onion-pepper mixture. Stir in chicken broth and cook and stir until mixture boils and is thickened. Add lemon juice, marmalade, and salt and pepper to taste. Stir in lobster meat. Spoon into a flat, buttered 1-quart casserole. Sprinkle with buttered crumbs. Bake at 400°F for 15 minutes or until hot and bubbly.
Yield: 6 servings

mother's salmon casserole

Delicious made with either pink or red salmon, this is a fast dish to prepare and keep in the refrigerator until it is time to pop it in the oven.

1 can (15½ ounces) pink salmon
18 single soda crackers
1 large rib celery
¼ green pepper
1 small onion

8 to 10 sprigs parsley
2 eggs
Milk
½ teaspoon salt
Fresh ground pepper to taste

Drain salmon, reserving liquid. Pick out bones and skin and flake salmon coarsely.

Lock bowl in position. Insert **steel blade**. Break crackers into 2 pieces and process until coarsely crushed. Put aside. Clean celery and cut into 1'' pieces. Remove seeds from green pepper and cut into several pieces. Peel onion and cut into fourths. Combine vegetable and parsley in processor and, with **steel blade**, process until finely chopped.

Layer crackers, salmon, and vegetables in a buttered 6-cup casserole, ending with crackers. Combine eggs, milk, and salmon liquid to make about a cup, with seasonings in processor and process just to blend. Pour over salmon in casserole. Dot top with butter. Bake at 350°F for 50 minutes or until set in center.
Yield: 4 servings

fish quenelles

The delightful fish "dumplings" called quenelles can be prepared from end pieces of fish. If you have not made them before, you will be surprised at their lovely, light, feathery texture.

2 slices white bread	½ teaspoon fresh ground nutmeg
½ cup hot milk	1 egg
½ pound fresh white fish	1 egg yolk
3 tablespoons butter	½ cup flour
½ teaspoon salt	Parslied Veloute Sauce

Lock bowl in position. Insert **steel blade**. Add bread and process until crumbs are formed. Empty into small bowl and combine with hot milk. Remove all skin and bones from fish and cut into 1″ to 2″ pieces. Process with **steel blade** until fish is pureed. Through the chute, add bread and milk, butter, salt, nutmeg, egg, and egg yolk, and process to blend. Chill.

To cook, shape chilled mixture into oval shapes with 2 dessert spoons and dip in flour. Place in a large buttered skillet. Gently pour boiling water into skillet to cover quenelles and cook below boiling point for about 8 to 10 minutes. Serve hot with parslied veloute sauce (below).
Yield: 4 servings

Parslied Veloute Sauce

4 or 5 sprigs parsley	1 cup hot fish court bouillon or
2 tablespoons butter or margarine	hot clam broth
2 tablespoons flour	Salt and pepper to taste

Lock bowl in position. Insert **steel blade**. Add parsley, butter, and flour, and process until blended. Slowly add hot liquid through the chute and process until smooth. Pour into a small saucepan and cook and stir until thickened. Season to taste.
Yield: 1 cup

gefilte fish

Traditionally served at the Passover seder, these fish balls are a welcome main dish any time of year. You can make them small and serve them with horseradish as appetizers. With the food processor grinding up the fish, it's fun to make your own fresh gefilte fish.

1 pound whitefish
2 pounds pike
3 medium onions, peeled
1 quart water
2 teaspoons salt

6 to 8 peppercorns
2 medium eggs
6 tablespoons ice water
1½ tablespoons matzo or cracker meal
2 carrots, peeled

Have fish filleted but save bones and head. Any combination of fresh water fish may be used.

Combine head, skin, bones, and 2 onions with 3 cups of water, 1 teaspoon salt, and peppercorns. Bring to a boil and simmer, covered, for at least 45 minutes, while preparing gefilte fish.

To make gefilte fish balls, cut remaining onion into quarters. Cut fish into 1" x 4" pieces. Lock bowl in position. Insert **steel blade**. Process fish 1 cup at a time and a piece of onion until finely ground. Remove to a mixing bowl. Combine eggs, water, and matzo meal in processor and process until blended. Add to ground fish and mix. If necessary to make a firm mixture, add additional meal. Shape into balls about 1½" in diameter.

Strain fish stock, discarding bones, etc., and put liquid in a saucepan. Bring to a boil. Add fish balls carefully and cover. Simmer for 1½ hours. Uncover for the last 30 minutes.

Lock bowl in position. Insert **slicing disc**. Slice carrots. Add to fish balls at end of 1 hour. At end of cooking time, taste and correct seasonings. Let fish cool a little and then spoon into a large rimmed platter. Arrange carrot slices around fish. Pour liquid over fish and chill.

Yield: 6 servings

fish fillets tampa

Try this unusual combination. Rice, hot and fluffy, would be a good partner.

4 slices dry bread
¼ teaspoon salt
Fresh ground pepper to taste
¼ teaspoon paprika

1½ pounds boneless fillets of cod or haddock
2 eggs
2 tablespoons water
Butter or margarine

Bread bread into pieces. Lock bowl in position. Insert **steel blade**. Put bread, salt, pepper, and paprika into work bowl and process to fine crumbs. Put into a flat plate. Cut fish fillets into 4 servings. Process eggs and water for a few seconds to blend. Pour into pie plate. Dip fish in egg and then in crumbs, coating all sides. Heat butter in skillet and cook fish until nicely browned on all sides. Serve with sauce.

Sauce

¼ medium green pepper, seeds removed
Peel from a navel orange
1 can (6 ounces) frozen orange juice concentrate

½ cup sugar
½ cup catsup
1½ tablespoons cornstarch
1 cup water

Cut green pepper and orange rind into 1" squares. Lock bowl in position. Insert **steel blade**. Combine all ingredients in processor and process until blended. Pour into a small saucepan and cook and stir until mixture boils. Lower heat and cook about 5 minutes until sauce thickens and is clear. Serve hot with fish.
Yield: About 2 cups

lamb with a crust

This is a special recipe for a special occasion.

4 to 6 pound leg of lamb roast
Salt and fresh ground pepper
    to taste
3 slices firm white bread

3 medium bay leaves
2 cloves garlic, peeled
4 tablespoons softened butter
1 cup dry white wine

Remove all fat from lamb. Place on a rack in a flat roasting pan and sprinkle with salt and pepper.

    Lock bowl in position. Insert **steel blade**. Break bread into pieces and put into processor with bay leaves and garlic. Spread lamb with butter and press crumbs into butter. Roast at 325°F for about 3 hours for medium. Remove from pan and let roast stand 15 to 20 minutes before slicing. Meanwhile, put wine in roasting pan and heat and scrape any residue from pan. Serve as pan gravy with lamb.

Yield: 6 servings with leftovers

veal loaf

When using veal, bone out the less expensive cuts. Be sure to use the bones to make meat stock.

1½ pounds boneless veal
½ pound fresh boneless pork
8 round butter crackers
1 small onion
2 eggs

½ cup catsup
1 tablespoon prepared mustard
1 teaspoon salt
Fresh ground pepper to taste
1 cup dairy sour cream

Cut veal and pork into 1'' cubes and mix together. Lock bowl in position. Insert **steel blade**. Process meat 1 cup at a time until finely chopped. After processing, remove to a bowl. When meat is processed, add remaining ingredients except sour cream and process with **steel blade** until blended. Add to meat in bowl and mix lightly to blend. Pack into a greased 9'' x 5'' x 2'' loaf pan. Bake at 350°F about 1½ to 2 hours.

    Remove from pan to a platter and let stand 10 minutes before cutting. Meanwhile, mix sour cream with pan juices and heat, but do not boil. Serve with veal loaf.

Yield: 8 servings

lamb pie

Meat pie recipes always sound complicated, but once you get the hang of them, they go together quickly. This recipe could also be made with leftover roast lamb.

2 pounds boneless lamb shoulder
¼ cup flour
½ teaspoon salt
Fresh ground pepper to taste
2 tablespoons butter or margarine
2 cups water
1 cup dry white wine
1/8 teaspoon leaf thyme
2 medium onions, peeled
2 ribs celery
4 medium carrots, peeled
Parsley Thyme Biscuits

Cut lamb into 2'' cubes, removing as much of the fat as possible. Mix flour with salt and pepper and coat lamb cubes with flour. Heat butter in large saucepan and brown lamb. Add water and wine and bring to a boil. Cover, reduce heat, and simmer about 30 minutes.

Lock bowl in position. Insert **slicer disc**. Cut onion to fit chute and slice. Wash and cut celery to fit chute and slice. Add to lamb. Cut carrots into 2'' pieces and add to lamb. Continue cooking until lamb and carrots are tender.

When lamb is cooked, transfer it and vegetables to a large casserole. Blend 1 cup liquid from lamb with 2 tablespoons flour in processor using **plastic blade**. Return to remaining liquid and cook and stir until mixture boils. Taste and correct seasoning. Pour over lamb in casserole.

Top with parsley thyme biscuits and bake at 400°F for 20 to 25 minutes or until biscuits are browned.
Yield: 6 servings

Parsley Thyme Biscuits

4 to 5 sprigs parsley
2 cups all-purpose flour
3 teaspoons baking powder
1 teaspoon salt
½ teaspoon leaf thyme
4 tablespoons chilled shortening
¾ cup milk, approximately

Lock bowl in position. Insert **steel blade**. Process parsley until coarsely chopped. Add dry ingredients. Cut shortening into small pieces and add to flour. Process until blended to a fine mixture. While still processing, add milk through chute. When mixture forms a ball, stop adding milk and stop processor. Turn out on a floured board. Pat dough ½'' thick. Cut into biscuits and put on top of stew.

pork chops baked with stuffing

Stuffing and meat combinations are fun to make when the food processor does the work.

1 rib celery
1 medium onion, peeled
3 to 4 sprigs parsley
½ teaspoon leaf sage
3 medium apples, peeled and cored
1 teaspoon salt

Fresh ground pepper to taste
6 slices bread
6 tablespoons butter, melted
6 pork chops
½ cup dry white wine

Wash celery and cut into 1'' pieces. Cut onion into fourths. Lock bowl in position. Insert **steel blade**. Add celery, onion, parsley, and sage to work bowl and process until medium coarse. Cut apples into 1'' cubes and add to vegetables with salt and pepper. Process until apples are chopped fine and mixture blended. Remove from bowl. Tear bread into pieces and process with **steel blade** to make coarse crumbs. Mix with vegetables and 3 tablespoons of butter.

Heat remaining butter in skillet and brown chops quickly on both sides. Spoon stuffing into a greased, flat, 2-quart casserole. Arrange chops on top of stuffing. Heat wine in skillet, scraping brown crust from bottom. Pour over chops in casserole. Cover casserole and bake at 350°F for 1 to 1½ hours. Remove cover during the last 10 minutes.
Yield: 6 servings

mushroom sauce

This is a pleasantly-flavored mushroom sauce when you need a gravy. Serve with meats.

½ pound medium mushrooms
¼ cup butter or margarine
1 medium onion
1 cup beef bouillon

1 tablespoon flour
1 tablespoon sherry wine
Salt and fresh ground pepper to taste

Lock bowl in position. Insert **slicer disc**. Cut off tough ends of mushrooms and rinse. Slice. Heat butter in a saucepan and gently saute mushrooms about 5 minutes. Meanwhile, insert **steel blade** in processor. Cut onion into fourths, process until finely chopped. Add remaining ingredients except salt and pepper and process to blend. Pour into cooked mushrooms and cook and stir until mixture boils and is thickened. Taste and correct seasonings.
Yield: About 2 cups

pork and vegetable casserole

This makes a wonderful football-season dish. It can be prepared in advance, refrigerated, and heated when needed. Add 20 to 30 minutes to time. If you feel adventuresome, add some basil, thyme, and marjoram.

1½ pounds boneless, lean pork
1 large green pepper
2 large onions, peeled
4 stalks celery
4 tablespoons butter or margerine
1 can (1 pound, 13 ounces) tomatoes

1½ teaspoon salt
Fresh ground pepper to taste
8 ounces noodles, cooked, drained
4 ounces American cheese
1 slice dry bread

Lock bowl in position. Insert **steel blade**. Cut pork into 1'' cubes and process 1 cup at a time until finely chopped. Remove from bowl after each processing. Remove seeds and white ribs from pepper and cut into 1'' squares. Cut onions into eighths. Wash celery and cut into 1'' pieces. Process vegetables with **steel blade** until coarsely chopped. Heat butter in a large skillet and lightly brown vegetables and pork. Add tomatoes and salt and pepper and cook 10 minutes.

Remove **steel blade** and insert **shredder disc**. Cut cheese to fit chute and grate cheese. Remove cheese from bowl and grate bread.

In a 2-quart buttered casserole, layer noodles, pork and vegetable mixture, and cheese, saving about ¼ cup of cheese to mix with crumbs for top. When all pork and noodles are layered, sprinkle cheese and crumbs on top. Bake at 350°F for 45 minutes or until bubbly.
Yield: 6 servings

cold orange sauce

This sauce is good with poultry, ham, or roast pork. Make it ahead of time and store in a covered container in the refrigerator. It will keep 2 or 3 days.

Thin yellow peel from 2 oranges
½ cup currant jelly
5 tablespoons sugar

¼ cup tawny port wine
¼ teaspoon salt
¼ cup orange juice

Lock bowl in position. Insert **steel blade**. Put in orange peel and process until finely chopped. Remove **steel blade** and insert **plastic blade**. Add remaining ingredients and process until blended and sugar dissolved.
Yield: About 1¼ cups

sausage patties

Tastes vary as to the best way to flavor sausage, so this recipe is deliberately simple. After you have made the recipe as it is, you may want to vary the seasonings as suggested at the end of the recipe. The marvelous thing about the food processor is being able to make your own dishes just as you like them.

1 pound boneless, fresh pork, ¼ of which should be pork fat
½ teaspoon salt
1½ teaspoons poultry seasoning

¼ teaspoon dried leaf sage, rubbed
Fresh ground pepper to taste
2 tablespoons water

Cut pork and fat into 1'' cubes and sprinkle with seasonings. Lock bowl in position. Insert **steel blade**. Process 1 cup of meat at a time until chopped fine, sprinkling a little water through chute while processing each cup. Mix pork fat with pork in each batch, so when the sausage is all processed it will be blended, and no additional mixing will be necessary. As each cup is processed, remove to another bowl. It will keep several days under refrigeration, or about 2 months at 0°F when freezer wrapped.
Yield: 1 pound of sausage

To cook sausage, form 1 pound into 6 flat patties. Pan fry over moderate heat, turning until nicely browned on both sides.
Yield: 3 to 4 servings

Italian Sausage: Use 1½ teaspoons Italian seasoning in place of poultry seasoning. For a "hotter" flavor, add ½ teaspoon Tabasco sauce.

sausage macaroni casserole

Even in a macaroni casserole, the food processor does almost everything but the cooking.

2 slices bread
2 ounces sharp Cheddar cheese
1 large onion
1 pound processor sausage
    (see page 84)
1½ cups milk

1 egg
1 teaspoon salt
Fresh ground pepper to taste
8 ounces elbow macaroni cooked,
    drained

Lock bowl in place. Insert **steel blade**. Tear bread into pieces and cut cheese into cubes. Process until finely chopped and blended. Remove from work bowl and reserve. Peel onion and cut into eighths. Add to work bowl and process until finely chopped with **steel blade**. Combine with sausage and fry until sausage is browned and onion is tender. Put milk, egg, salt, and pepper in work bowl and process with **steel blade** a few seconds until blended. Combine milk mixture, sausage, onion, and macaroni and spoon into a buttered 6-cup casserole. Sprinkle with crumbs and cheese. Bake at 350°F for 30 to 40 minutes or until center is set.
Yield: 4 to 6 servings

spaghetti sauce

This sauce dresses spaghetti to perfection.

1 large onion
1 large rib celery
1 carrot
1 clove garlic
6 sprigs parsley
2 tablespoons butter
2 tablespoons olive oil
2 tablespoons bacon fat

1 pound lean beef
1 can (2 or 2½ pounds) crushed,
    peeled tomatoes in puree
½ teaspoon fresh thyme leaves or
    ¼ teaspoon dried thyme leaves
1 teaspoon salt
Fresh ground pepper to taste

Peel onion and cut into 8 pieces. Wash celery and cut into 1'' pieces. Peel carrot and cut into 1'' lengths. Peel garlic. Lock bowl in position. Insert **steel blade**.

Add vegetables, including parsley, and process a few seconds until chopped medium fine. Heat butter, oil, and bacon fat in a large skillet. Add vegetables and saute slowly.

Cut meat into 1'' cubes and process with **steel blade**, 1 cup at a time, until chopped medium fine. Add to vegetables in skillet and saute until pink color is gone. Add tomatoes and seasonings. Cover and cook slowly; stirring occasionally, 1 to 2 hours. Serve hot over cooked spaghetti.

Yield: 4 servings

vegetable sauce for spaghetti

This is a wonderfully flavorful sauce of garden vegetables to serve on spaghetti as a main dish.

1 medium onion
1 clove garlic
3 medium-to-large zucchinis
1 carrot
3 medium tomatoes
1 teaspoon salt
Fresh ground pepper to taste
2 teaspoons chopped fresh basil
　　　or 1 teaspoon dried

1 teaspoon fresh leaf oregano or
　　½ teaspoon dried
½ teaspoon fresh leaf thyme or
　　¼ teaspoon dried
2 tablespoons olive oil
1 tablespoon butter
6 ounces Parmesan cheese
Hot cooked spaghetti

Peel onion and cut into eighths. Peel garlic. Cut off stem end of zucchinis and cut to fit chute. Peel carrot and cut to fit chute. Peel tomatoes and cut to fit chute. Lock bowl in position. Insert **steel blade**. Chop onion and garlic fine. Remove **steel blade** and insert **shredder disc**. Shred vegetables. As work bowl fills up, remove vegetables to a large bowl. Don't lose any of the juice. When done, add seasonings and mix lightly.

　　　Heat olive oil and butter in a large skillet. Add vegetables and saute quickly over medium heat. Reduce heat and simmer 15 minutes or less. While vegetables are cooking, lock bowl in position and insert **steel disc**. Cut Parmesan cheese into 1'' cubes and process a few at a time to make 1 cup. Serve sauce on hot spaghetti with generous spoonfuls of Parmesan cheese.

Yield: 4 servings

veal lombardy

Try this with hot steamed rice.

2 pounds leg of veal, cut into
  1" cubes
2 tablespoons olive oil
4 tablespoons butter
1 cup water
1 beef bouillon cube
1 cup Chablis wine
2 tablespoons flour

1 teaspoon salt
Fresh ground pepper to taste
2 medium yellow onions, peeled
½ pound mushrooms
4 tomatoes
1 clove garlic
6 sprigs parsley

Brown veal in olive oil and half of the butter. As veal browns, transfer to a 2-quart casserole which can be used on top of stove. When all veal is browned, add water, bouillon cube, and wine to skillet and cook. Stir to remove crust from skillet. Sprinkle flour on veal. Add liquid to veal in casserole and season with salt and pepper. Cover and simmer until almost tender, about 45 minutes.

Meanwhile, lock bowl in position. Insert **slicer disc**. Cut onions to fit chute and slice. Slice mushrooms. Remove **slicer disc** and insert **steel blade**. Cut tomatoes into quarters and process with garlic until coarsely chopped. Cook onions, mushrooms, tomatoes, and garlic in remaining butter for 10 minutes. Add to veal in casserole and continue cooking until veal is tender. Process parsley with **steel blade** to chop fine and sprinkle over casserole before serving.
Yield: 6 servings

Vegetables

Slicing, chopping, and shredding by the processor will save your hands and speed the work. You will soon learn how to prepare your own favorite vegetables with ease. When going through a series of preparations, remember that the processor doesn't have to be washed after every use. If you don't want to mix tomatoes and onions, rinse it out—which is a good habit to get into at the end of a job—then there's no dried-on food when you are ready to wash it.

Be sure the raw vegetables to be processed are cold and crisp.

stuffed artichokes

A very good first course or serve it as a luncheon entree with sliced chicken sandwiches.

6 artichokes
2 tablespoons lemon juice
2 teaspoons salt
4 slices dry bread
1 large onion, peeled
1 clove garlic, peeled

15 sprigs parsley
2 slices bacon, diced
Fresh ground pepper to taste
⅓ cup each water, dry red wine,
     and olive oil

Cut off stem end of artichoke to make a flat base. Cut 1'' off top of artichoke and remove 1 layer of outer leaves. Trim tips of leaves from outer 1 or 2 layers. Place artichokes in a saucepan which will hold them fairly snugly. Add lemon juice and 1 teaspoon salt. Cover with water, bring to a boil, and cook 15 minutes. Drain and cool. Remove choke from center of artichokes with a spoon or paring knife.

    Lock bowl in position. Insert **steel blade**. Break bread slices into 2 or 3 pieces and process to fine crumbs. Remove from work bowl and reserve.

    Cut onion into eighths and process onion, garlic, and parsley with **steel blade** until finely chopped.

    Cook bacon, onion, garlic, and parsley 8 to 10 minutes over low heat. Mix with bread crumbs, remaining teaspoon salt, and pepper.

    Put cooked artichokes top side down on a flat surface and press lightly with hand to open leaves. Turn artichokes over and fill center and between leaves with stuffing. Place in a large skillet with a domed lid and add water, wine, and olive oil. Cover and simmer 45 minutes. Chill to serve.

Yield: 6 servings

sauteed celery

This is a vegetable quickie that adds both texture and flavor to the meal.

6 ribs celery
1 medium onion, peeled
2 tablespoons butter

2 tablespoons water
Salt and fresh ground pepper to taste

Wash and trim celery. Cut into lengths to fit chute. Lock bowl in position. Insert **slicer disc**. Arrange celery in chute so curve fits curve. Slice. Cut onion to fit chute and slice. Combine all ingredients in a skillet or small saucepan. Cover tightly. Bring to a boil and simmer 2 to 3 minutes.

Yield: 4 servings

chinese vegetables

Crisp and flavorful, this dish is a nice accompaniment to easy Chinese chicken (see page 66).

2 medium carrots, peeled
3 stalks celery
¼ pound fresh mushrooms
2 scallions, cleaned
1 can (16 ounces) bean sprouts,
    drained

2 tablespoons salad oil
2 chicken bouillon cubes
1 cup hot water
1½ tablespoons cornstarch
2 tablespoons soy sauce

Cut carrots into pieces to fit chute. Wash celery and cut to fit chute. Trim tough ends from mushrooms. Lock bowl in position. Insert **slicer disc**. Fit carrots, celery, and mushrooms into chute and slice. As bowl becomes full, transfer to another bowl, keeping carrots separate. With a knife, cut both green and white parts of scallions into 1'' pieces. Heat oil in a large skillet or wok and stir-fry carrots for 5 minutes. Add remaining vegetables and stir-fry 2 to 3 minutes over medium-high heat. Dissolve chicken bouillon in hot water and add to vegetables. Mix cornstarch and soy sauce and stir into vegetables. Bring to a boil. Serve at once.
Yield: 6 servings

green rice souffle

This is a fine accompaniment to the meat course or it can almost stand on its own as a luncheon dish.

2 cups raw spinach leaves
1 medium onion
1 can (10¾ ounces) mushroom
    soup

3 eggs, separated
½ teaspoon salt
Fresh ground pepper to taste
3 cups cooked rice

Wash and crisp spinach leaves. Peel onion and cut into eighths. Lock bowl in position. Insert **steel blade**. Process spinach until finely chopped. Remove from processor. Add onion, soup, egg yolks, salt, pepper, and process until onion is chopped and mixture blended. Combine with spinach and rice. Beat egg whites until stiff and fold into rice mixture. Spoon into a well-buttered, 6-cup casserole. Bake at 350°F for 40 minutes or until firm.
Yield: 6 servings

french fried potatoes

*With the **French cutter disc**, white or sweet potatoes are quickly cut to fry in hot shortening or oil and add another personal touch to the meal. Many pieces of frying equipment are available that use minimum amounts of fat for frying, but an electric skillet also works.*

Peel white or sweet potatoes and cut to fit chute. Lock bowl in position. Insert **French cutter disc**. Process potatoes. Allow the equivalent of 1 medium potato per person to be served.

Heat oil or shortening to 400°F in a fryer or an electric skillet. If an electric skillet is used, have at least 2'' of fat. Use a fryer basket in a fryer—a slotted fork or spoon in an electric skillet to put the potatoes in and out of the fat. Fry 5 to 6 minutes or until golden. Remove potatoes from fat and drain on paper towels. Sprinkle with salt.

potato pancakes

Remember the chipped fingers from grating potatoes for potato pancakes? That's all gone with the food processor! Serve with sour cream or applesauce.

2 large potatoes, peeled
1 small onion, peeled
2 eggs
2 to 4 tablespoons milk
2 tablespoons butter, melted

¼ cup all-purpose flour
½ teaspoon salt
Fresh ground pepper to taste
Butter for frying
Dairy sour cream

Lock bowl in position. Insert **shredder disc**. Cut potatoes and onion to fit chute and grate. Remove to a medium-size mixing bowl. Remove **shredder disc** and insert **plastic blade**. Add eggs, milk, and melted butter and blend. Then add flour, salt, and pepper and process to mix. Pour over potatoes and onions in bowl and stir to mix together. Drop by quarter cupfuls on a buttered griddle or skillet. Spread to make a 4'' pancake. Cook until brown on both sides, turning.
Yield: 8 to 10 pancakes

potato vegetable bake

Bake a chicken at the same time.

3 tomatoes, peeled
2 medium onions
4 ribs celery
5 medium potatoes

1 teaspoon salt
Fresh ground pepper to taste
4 tablespoons butter or margarine

Cut tomatoes and onion to fit chute. Wash celery and cut to fit chute. Peel potatoes and cut to fit chute. Lock bowl in position. Insert **slicer disc**. Slice all vegetables, removing from work bowl and keeping separated as sliced. Arrange in layers in a buttered 6-cup casserole, beginning and ending with potatoes. Sprinkle each layer with salt and pepper. Dot top layer with butter. Cover and bake at 400°F for 45 to 50 minutes or until potatoes are tender. Uncover for the last 10 minutes to brown potatoes.
Yield: 6 servings

swiss roesti potatoes

Potatoes are often cooked this way in Switzerland. They are good for breakfast, lunch, or dinner.

4 medium potatoes
½ teaspoon salt

4 tablespoons shortening
2 tablespoons butter

Scrub potatoes and cook in boiling, salted water for 15 minutes. Drain and chill potatoes in refrigerator for several hours or overnight. Lock bowl in position. Insert **shredder disc**. Peel and cut potatoes to fit chute and shred, removing from bowl as it becomes full. Heat shortening and butter in a heavy skillet. Add potatoes and season to taste with salt and fresh ground pepper. Cook, uncovered, over moderate heat until underside is well browned. Turn to brown other side by holding plate over skillet, reverse skillet and plate, then slide potatoes from plate back into skillet to brown. Cut into wedges to serve.
Yield: 4 servings

country fries

With the food processor, it is so easy to slice potatoes for country fries that one must learn to resist the temptation to have them too often.

5 medium potatoes
1 medium onion
½ teaspoon salt

Fresh ground pepper to taste
3 tablespoons butter or margarine
3 tablespoons shortening

Peel potatoes and cut to fit chute. Peel onion and cut to fit chute. Lock bowl in position. Insert **slicer disc**. Feed potatoes and onions through chute until all are sliced. Season with salt and pepper. Heat butter and shortening in an 8'' to 9'' heavy skillet. Add potatoes and cook 20 to 30 minutes over moderate heat, turning. During cooking cover potatoes with a round piece of waxed paper cut to fit the skillet, and with a hole in the middle to allow steam to escape. Potatoes cut shoestring style can be fried in the same manner.
Yield: 4 servings

sweet potato-apple casserole

For a fine combination, bake this casserole at the same time you are roasting pork.

3 cups cooked, peeled, sweet
    potatoes, sliced 1" thick
2 slices white bread
¼ cup butter or margarine,
    softened

½ cup honey
Thin yellow peel of ½ orange
1½ cups peeled, cored, diced apples
½ teaspoon salt
2 tablespoons butter, softened

Arrange sweet potatoes in a buttered, 4-cup casserole. Lock bowl in position. Insert **steel blade**. Tear bread into pieces and process to make fine crumbs. Remove from bowl and set aside. Put ¼ cup butter, honey, orange peel, apples, and salt in bowl and process to blend. Pour over sweet potatoes. Sprinkle crumbs over sweet potatoes and dot with 2 tablespoons butter. Bake at 350°F for 1 hour.
Yield: 4 to 6 servings

eggplant deluxe

Eggplant deluxe is a truly good combination of flavors, especially good with wild game.

1 medium eggplant	**2 eggs**
6 medium fresh mushrooms	**¾ cup light cream**
3 tablespoons butter or margarine	**1 teaspoon salt**
1 small onion	**Fresh ground pepper to taste**
12 single soda crackers	

Peel eggplant and cut to fit chute. Cut off tough ends of mushroom stems. Lock bowl in position. Insert **French cutter**. Feed eggplant and mushrooms into chute to process. As work bowl fills, transfer to skillet with butter and saute eggplant and mushrooms over medium heat for 5 minutes. Remove **French cutter** and insert **steel blade**. Peel and quarter onion. Add to work bowl and process until chopped fine. Add remaining ingredients and process to blend.

Combine with eggplant and spoon into a greased 1-quart casserole. Bake at 375°F for 30 minutes or until set in center.
Yield: 4 servings

Note: If **French cutter** is not available, use **slicer disc**.

squash midori

This attractive, Italian-style dish tastes as good as it looks. Serve with beef or pork chopped in the processor.

1 medium onion	**½ teaspoon salt**
1 clove garlic	**Fresh ground pepper to taste**
2 medium yellow squash	**1 teaspoon chopped fresh basil or**
2 medium zucchinis	**½ teaspoon dried basil**
2 small, ripe tomatoes	**2 tablespoons butter or margarine**

Lock bowl in position. Insert **steel blade**. Cut onion into quarters and add with peeled garlic to bowl. Process to chop fine. Remove **steel blade** and insert **slicer disc**. Wash squash and zucchinis and cut off stem ends. If necessary, cut to fit chute. Slice into work bowl. Remove ingredients to a saucepan if bowl becomes too full. Slice tomatoes into bowl. Put into a saucepan and add remaining ingredients. Bring to a boil and simmer, covered, for 5 minutes.
Yield: 4 to 6 servings

mushroom souffle

Mushroom souffle will be good with almost any meat or poultry. The bread base makes it less fragile than the typical souffle.

6 slices bread
1 small onion
2 ribs celery
3 tablespoons butter or margarine
1 pound mushrooms

2 tablespoons lemon juice
3 eggs
1½ cups milk
¾ teaspoon salt
¼ teaspoon dried rosemary

Break bread slices into several pieces. Lock bowl in position. Insert **steel blade**. Process bread into coarse crumbs and remove from bowl and reserve. Peel onion and cut into several pieces. Wash celery and cut into 1'' pieces. Process with **steel blade** until finely chopped. Heat butter in large skillet and saute onions and celery over low heat until tender but not browned. Meanwhile, with **steel blade**, process mushrooms in several batches until finely chopped. Add mushrooms and lemon juice to onion-celery mixture in skillet and cook over low heat until all liquid is evaporated. Add bread crumbs and mix. Put eggs, milk, salt, and rosemary in bowl and process with **steel blade** until blended. Combine with mushrooms.

Spoon into a buttered 6-cup casserole and bake at 350°F for 45 minutes or until set in center.
Yield: 6 servings

bechamel sauce

Serve this sauce over hot vegetables such as cauliflower, carrots, onions, or green beans.

1 small onion
Celery leaves from 1 rib
2 tablespoons butter, softened
½ cup chicken broth

1 tablespoon flour
½ cup light cream
Salt and pepper to taste

Lock bowl in position. Insert **steel blade**. Process onion and celery leaves until chopped very fine. Add remaining ingredients and process to blend. Cook over moderate heat until thickened, stirring.
Yield: 1 cup

turnip croquettes

This is a new way to serve a winter vegetable.

2 slices dry bread
3 ounces Cheddar cheese
3 cups cooked turnips,
    diced

4 tablespoons melted butter or
    margarine
2 eggs
Fresh ground pepper to taste

Lock bowl in position. Insert **steel blade**. Process bread to fine crumbs. Remove from work bowl and reserve. Cut cheese into cubes. Add cheese cubes, turnips, butter, and 1 egg to processor. Process with **steel blade** until blended. Chill. Beat remaining egg slightly. Shape turnip mixture into 1'' balls. Dip in egg and in crumbs. Place on a well-greased cookie sheet and bake at 425°F for 15 to 20 minutes.
Yield: 6 servings

hollandaise sauce

Serve on asparagus or broccoli.

3 egg yolks
2 tablespoons lemon juice
½ teaspoon salt

Dash white pepper
½ cup butter, softened
½ cup boiling water

Lock bowl in position. Insert **plastic blade**. Put egg yolks, lemon juice, salt, pepper, and butter in bowl and process until blended. With processor operating, slowly pour in boiling water, processing until blended. Cook over hot water, stirring constantly, until mixture is thick and custard-like.
Yield: 1½ cups

herbed tomato noodles

Spoon this sauce over your homemade noodles. This would go nicely with any poultry dish.

1 recipe noodles (see page 116)
1 teaspoon fresh or ½ teaspoon
    dried basil
¼ teaspoon each fresh or pinch
    dried oregano and thyme

2 medium tomatoes
2 tablespoons softened butter or
    margarine
Fresh ground pepper to taste

Cook noodles in boiling, salted water about 10 minutes or until tender. While noodles are cooking, lock bowl in position. Insert **steel blade**. Wash tomatoes, remove stem end, and cut each into 4 pieces. Add with herbs, butter, and pepper to bowl and process until chopped medium fine. Saute mixture in a small skillet until heated through. Drain noodles and serve with tomatoes.
Yield: 4 servings

Salads and Salad Dressings

The incredible variety of salad dressings which can be prepared in moments in the processor will give you a real repertoire without resorting to commercial mixes. The delicate mayonnaise which can be made in small or larger batches enhances any food with which it is used.

Remember that the processor chops, slices, or shreds much better when vegetables are cold and crisp and fruits cold and not overripe.

processor mayonnaise

This is a delicate mayonnaise. The recipe may be cut in half if desired.

2 eggs
1 teaspoon salt
1 teaspoon dry mustard

4 tablespoons lemon juice or vinegar
2 cups salad oil

Lock bowl in position. Insert **steel blade**. Put eggs, salt, mustard, lemon juice, and ⅓ cup oil in work bowl. Process about 15 seconds. Add remaining oil through the chute in a slow stream while processing. After all oil is added, process about 15 seconds more. Store in a covered container in the refrigerator.
Yield: 2½ cups

Curry Mayonnaise: Add 1½ teaspoons curry powder and ½ cup chopped coconut to 1 cup mayonnaise. Use as a dressing for fruit salad.

Carrot Mayonnaise: Peel and cut 2 carrots into 1'' pieces. Process with **steel blade** until chopped very fine. A small piece of onion may be added to process with carrot, if desired. Fold into 1 cup mayonnaise. Use with either vegetables or fruit.

cucumbers in marinade

Prepare this refreshing dish in advance to add flavor to salads.

½ cup salad oil
¼ cup vinegar
1½ teaspoons sugar
½ teaspoon salt

Fresh ground pepper to taste
1 onion, peeled
2 cucumbers, peeled

Combine oil, vinegar, sugar, salt, and pepper in a bowl. Cut onion to fit chute. Lock bowl in position. Insert **slicer disc**. Slice onion. Remove from bowl. Slice cucumbers. Add cucumbers and onions to oil-vinegar mixture in alternate layers. Cover and chill well. Add to mixed vegetable salads as needed. Will keep up to 1 week.
Yield: About 2 cups

basic french dressing

There are many easy variations of this tasty dressing.

1 cup salad oil
5 tablespoons vinegar or lemon
 juice
1 teaspoon salt

2 teaspoons paprika
1 teaspoon dry mustard
1 teaspoon Worcestershire sauce
Fresh ground pepper to taste

Lock bowl in position. Insert **plastic blade**. Add all ingredients and process to blend.
Yield: 1⅓ cups. For the dressing recipes which follow, insert **steel blade**.

French Garlic Dressing: Add 1 clove garlic, peeled, and process.

French Parsley Dressing: Add 1 small onion, peeled and cut into quarters, and 1 cup loosely packed fresh parsley. Process.

French Roquefort Dressing: Add 2 ounces Roquefort cheese after other ingredients have been processed. Process on MOMENTARY.

French Herb Dressing: Add 2 teaspoons crushed basil, ½ teaspoon dried leaf thyme, and 1/8 teaspoon dried leaf rosemary.

vinaigrette sauce

Vinaigrette sauce is particularly good on cold, cooked asparagus salad, but it is good, too, with chilled, cooked green beans or as a dressing for lettuce wedges.

1 small gherkin
6 medium stuffed olives
10 chive stems
½ teaspoon dry mustard
1 teaspoon Worcestershire sauce

½ teaspoon salt
Fresh ground pepper to taste
⅓ cup tarragon vinegar
1 cup salad oil

Cut gherkin into several pieces, olives in half, and chives into 1'' lengths. Lock bowl in position. Insert **steel blade**. Add all ingredients and process a few seconds until pickles, olives, and chives are chopped and ingredients blended. Chill well before using.
Yield: About 1½ cups

basic creamy dressing

The food processor combines the ingredients so the dressing stays creamy to the last drop. The seasoning variations of this recipe are infinite.

1 cup salad oil
⅓ cup vinegar
2 cloves garlic
1 teaspoon dry mustard

1 teaspoon Worcestershire sauce
½ cup mayonnaise
½ teaspoon salt
Fresh ground pepper to taste

Lock bowl in position. Insert **steel blade**. Add all ingredients and process several seconds until blended.
Yield: 1¾ cups

Creamy Tomato Dressing: Add 3 tablespoons catsup or tomato sauce and 1/8 teaspoon each of oregano, basil, and thyme with other ingredients.

Creamy Herb Dressing: Add 3 tablespoons mixed fresh herbs with other ingredients.

Creamy Roquefort Dressing: Add 4 tablespoons Roquefort cheese with other ingredients.

Creamy Olive Dressing: Add ¼ cup stuffed olives with other ingredients.

celery seed dressing

This dressing is very good for fruit salad.

½ cup sugar
¼ cup vinegar
1/8 teaspoon salt
¼ teaspoon dry mustard

1 teaspoon paprika
1 cup salad oil
1 teaspoon celery seed

Combine sugar, vinegar, salt, mustard, and paprika in a saucepan. Bring to a boil, stirring. Cool. Lock bowl in position. Insert **plastic blade**. Add cooled sugar mixture. Add oil through chute while processing. When blended, add celery seed.
Yield: 1½ cups

tangy vegetable dressing

¼ green pepper
1 clove garlic
1 small onion
1 tablespoon Worcestershire sauce
1 teaspoon dry mustard
1 teaspoon salt

1 tablespoon sugar
1 can (10¾ ounces) condensed
    tomato soup
½ cup cider vinegar
1½ cups salad oil

Remove seeds and white ribs from pepper. Cut into 1'' strips. Peel garlic and cut into two pieces. Lock bowl in position. Insert **steel blade**. Combine all ingredients in bowl and process until blended. Use as a dressing for vegetable salads. Keep chilled in refrigerator.
Yield: About 3½ cups

Thousand Island Dressing: Combine 1 cup mayonnaise with 1 cup vegetable dressing. Add 3 tablespoons pickle relish and 1 hard-cooked egg, chopped.
Yield: 2 cups

cran-apple-orange delight

This salad-relish can be served as is or try the other serving suggestions included in the recipe.

1 navel orange
1 apple

1 pound (4 cups) cranberries
1 cup sugar

Cut orange in quarters lengthwise and remove seeds, if any. Cut each quarter into 2 pieces. Peel apple, quarter, and remove core. Lock bowl in position. Insert **steel blade**. Partially process orange and apple before adding the cranberries. Process until mixture is coarsely chopped. Store in refrigerator for a day to blend flavors.
Yield: 3¼ cups

Note: For variation, ½ cup uncut walnuts or pecans can be added with fruits. Serve as a relish or make a beautiful and flavorful salad by placing 2 pear halves, cut side up, on shredded lettuce. Fill center with cottage cheese and add Cran-Apple-Orange Delight.

herbed yogurt dressing

You will find this dressing especially tasty with salad greens.

2 slices onion
6 sprigs parsley
½ teaspoon tarragon leaves
1 clove garlic
3 tablespoons salad oil

½ teaspoon salt
Fresh ground pepper to taste
1 teaspoon vinegar
1 cup plain yogurt

Lock bowl in position. Insert **steel blade**. Put onion, parsley, tarragon, garlic, and salad oil in bowl and process until blended. Remove **steel blade**. Insert **plastic blade**. Add salt, pepper, vinegar, and yogurt. Process until just blended. Chill well for several hours.
Yield: About 1½ cups

cottage cheese aspic

Cottage cheese aspic can be served on lettuce as a dinner salad or for lunch, combined with shrimp or tuna salad.

1½ cups tomato juice
1 package (4 servings) lemon-
        flavored gelatin
½ cup mayonnaise

1 cup large or small curd cottage
        cheese
1 teaspoon onion salt

Heat ½ cup tomato juice to boiling. Combine with gelatin and stir to dissolve. Lock bowl in position. Insert **steel blade.** Combine remaining ingredients in bowl and process until smooth. Add dissolved gelatin and process for a few seconds to blend. Spoon into a quart ring-mold or pan. Refrigerate until firm.
Yield: 4 to 6 servings

fruit salad dressing

1 ripe banana
½ cup pineapple juice
½ cup salad oil

½ teaspoon salt
1 tablespoon lemon juice
½ cup yogurt

Lock bowl in position. Insert **plastic blade**. Peel banana and cut into chunks. Add to bowl with remaining ingredients. Process until blended.
Yield: About 1½ cups

cole slaw

This is a base for a cole slaw recipe. It is easy to add or change ingredients. For instance, cucumbers can be used in place of radishes, slice up a tomato in the processor, or add parsley.

1 carrot, peeled
2 ribs celery, cleaned
1 small onion or 1 green onion
3 or 4 radishes
½ small crisp cabbage

½ cup mayonnaise
2 tablespoons French dressing
½ teaspoon salt
Fresh ground pepper to taste

Lock bowl in position. Insert **steel blade**. Cut carrot, celery, and onion into 1" pieces. Halve radishes. Add to bowl. Process on MOMENTARY until medium-fine. Remove to a bowl. Remove **steel blade** and insert **slicer disc**. Cut cabbage to fit chute and process to slice. Add to vegetables. Add remaining ingredients and stir to mix.
Yield: About 4 cups

jellied vegetable salad

This salad fits into many menus—particularly welcome in the winter.

1 envelope unflavored gelatin
¼ cup cold water
1 cup water
2 tablespoons lemon juice
½ teaspoon salt
1 teaspoon sugar

1 carrot, peeled
1 small wedge cabbage
2 ribs celery
½ medium green pepper
1 small onion

Soften gelatin in cold water. Dissolve over hot water. Combine water, lemon juice, salt, and sugar with gelatin. Chill until mixture begins to thicken.

Cut carrot into 1" pieces. Cut cabbage coarsely. Wash celery and cut into 1" pieces. Remove seeds and white rib from green pepper and cut into 1" squares. Cut onion into fourths.

Lock bowl in position. Insert **steel blade**. Add vegetables and process with on/off motion until medium-coarsely chopped. Fold into thickened gelatin. Spoon into a 3-cup mold. Chill until firm. Serve on lettuce with mayonnaise.
Yield: 4 to 6 servings

spring cucumber mold

Here's a lovely-looking vegetable mold to dress up your buffet table. It's zingy flavor complements any fish or meat.

3 envelopes unflavored gelatin
½ teaspoon salt
2 tablespoons sugar
4 tablespoons white vinegar
2 cups hot water
1 small onion, peeled

5" piece of horseradish root
    (or 2 tablespoons com-
    mercial horseradish)
2 large cucumbers, peeled
1 cup dairy sour cream
½ cucumber, unpeeled

Combine gelatin, salt, sugar, and vinegar. Add hot water and stir until gelatin is dissolved. Put into the refrigerator to chill, stirring occasionally until mixture begins to thicken.

    Meanwhile, lock bowl in position. Insert **shredder disc**. Shred onion, horseradish, and peeled cucumbers. Combine shredded vegetables and sour cream with thickened gelatin and spoon into a 6-cup mold. Chill several hours or overnight. Unmold on platter. Fill center with additional sour cream. Slice unpeeled cucumber with **slicer disc** and garnish around mold with slices.
Yield: 8 to 10 servings

shrimp remoulade

This New Orleans dish may also be served as a first course.

1 rib celery
2 green onions
½ green pepper
¾ cup sharp prepared mustard
½ cup catsup

¾ cup salad oil
½ cup vinegar
1½ pounds cooked, chilled shrimp
Shredded lettuce

Clean celery and onion and cut into 1'' pieces (use green and white part of onion). Remove seeds and white rib from pepper and cut into 1'' pieces. Lock bowl in position. Insert **steel blade**. Process celery, onion, and green pepper medium-fine. Add mustard, catsup, salad oil, and vinegar and process just to blend. Pour over shrimp and refrigerate several hours. Drain sauce from shrimp. Serve on shredded lettuce as a salad.
Yield: 4 servings

Breads, Pancakes, Dumplings, and Biscuits

All kinds of baked items can be prepared in the food processor with the greatest of ease. There are a few basic rules to remember.

Do not overprocess. Generally, unless otherwise directed, process just until the dry ingredients are moistened.

Do not dig in around the **steel blade** with a spatula when removing a batter. Pull out the **steel blade**, clean it off with a spatula, and remove the remaining batter. The **steel blade** can then be repositioned, if necessary.

Nuts can be added in the first processing period, as they will be chopped sufficiently when the product is ready for baking.

If dough does not leave the side of the bowl cleanly during the processing, add 1 or 2 tablespoons flour through the chute and process 1 or 2 seconds.

white bread

Nicely textured; make several loaves in quick succession to bake at once. You will be pleased with the result.

¾ cup milk
1 package active dry yeast
1½ tablespoons sugar
3 cups all-purpose flour

1 teaspoon salt
2 tablespoons chilled butter or
    margarine

Heat milk to lukewarm. Add yeast and sugar. Stir and let stand for 5 minutes. Lock bowl in position. Insert **steel blade**. Add flour, salt, and butter cut into pieces. Process 1 or 2 seconds until butter is blended with flour. Add yeast mixture through chute and process until dough forms a ball. Remove dough to a floured surface and cut into 2 pieces. Break each half into 3 or 4 pieces and press against **steel blade**. Process until dough forms a ball. Break apart and process again. Repeat with other half of dough. Combine both halves in a buttered bowl and butter dough on all sides. Cover with wax paper and a towel and let rise in a warm place until doubled in bulk, about 1 hour. Punch down and shape into 1 or 2 loaves. Bake 1 loaf in a greased 9'' x 5'' x 3'' loaf pan or 2 loaves in 7-3/4'' x 3-5/8'' x 2-1/4'' loaf pans. (These pans are sometimes sold as 1-pound meat loaf pans.) Cover and let rise again until doubled in bulk. Bake at 400°F for 30 minutes or until golden brown. Remove from pan at once and cool on rack, covered with a towel. If desired, the hot bread may be brushed with butter.
Yield: 1 large or 2 smaller loaves

toasted cheese bread

This French bread zips up a meal and is a wonderful addition to a fruit salad lunch.

2 ounces sharp Cheddar cheese,
    chilled
4 tablespoons chilled butter

¼ cup sesame seeds
1 loaf French bread, split lengthwise

Lock bowl in position. Insert **shredder disc**. Cut chilled cheese to fit chute and process to grate. Remove **shredder disc** and insert **steel blade**. Cut chilled butter in 6 to 8 pieces and arrange over cheese. Add sesame seeds. Process a few seconds until blended. Spread both cut sides of French bread with cheese mixture. Bake at 400°F for 10 minutes or until heated through. Cut crosswise into pieces and serve at once.
Yield: 6 servings

apple wheat bread

Try this not-too-sweet "wheaty" bread.

¾ cup walnut meats
1 cup peeled, cored, quartered
    apples
1 cup all-purpose flour
2 teaspoons baking powder
½ teaspoon soda
1 teaspoon salt

1¾ cup whole wheat flour
½ cup wheat germ
5 tablespoons brown sugar
2 eggs
4 tablespoons salad oil
1 cup buttermilk

Lock bowl in position. Insert **steel blade**. Add ingredients to bowl in order given. Process just until mixture is blended. Spoon into a greased 9'' x 5'' x 2'' loaf pan. Bake at 350°F for 1 hour or until a cake tester inserted in center of loaf comes out clean. Cool in pan 10 minutes. Cool on rack. When cool, wrap in aluminum foil and store overnight. If bread is not used immediately, store in refrigerator.
Yield: 1 loaf

french bread

1 cup lukewarm water
1 package active dry yeast
2 tablespoons sugar
3 cups all-purpose flour

1 teaspoon salt
2 tablespoons chilled butter or
    margarine

Combine water, yeast, and sugar. Stir and let stand 5 minutes. Lock bowl in position. Insert **steel blade**. Add flour, salt, and butter cut into pieces. Process 1 or 2 seconds, until butter is blended with flour. Add yeast mixture through chute and process until dough forms a ball. Remove dough to a floured surface and cut into 2 pieces. Break each half into 3 or 4 pieces and press against **steel blade**. Process until dough forms a ball. Break apart and process again. Repeat with other half of dough. Combine both halves in a buttered bowl and butter dough on all sides. Cover with wax paper and a towel and let rise in a warm place until doubled in bulk, about 1 hour. Punch down. Divide dough in half. Roll on floured board into a rectangle about 16'' x 6''. Roll up from long side to form a long loaf and transfer to a greased baking sheet. Repeat with other half. With a scissors cut gashes crosswise, about 2'' apart. Sprinkle top of loaf lightly with flour. Cover and let rise in a warm place until doubled in bulk. Bake at 400°F for 30 to 35 minutes or until bread is brown and crusty. If desired, a pan of boiling water can be put in oven with bread while it is baking.
Yield: 2 loaves

whole wheat bread

Here is a recipe sure to please those who prefer a whole wheat bread.

1 cup milk
1 package active dry yeast
1½ tablespoons brown sugar
1 cup all-purpose white flour

2 cups whole wheat flour
1½ teaspoons salt
1 tablespoon chilled butter or
    margarine

Heat milk to lukewarm. Stir in yeast and sugar and let stand 5 minutes. Lock bowl in position. Insert **steel blade**. Put flours and salt in bowl. Cut butter into small pieces and add to bowl. Process until blended. With processor running add milk-yeast mixture. Process until dough forms a ball. Remove dough to a floured surface and cut into 2 pieces. Break each half into 3 or 4 pieces and press against **steel blade**. Process until dough forms a ball. Break apart and process again.
    Repeat with other half of dough. Combine 2 kneaded portions and place in a buttered bowl. Turn dough in bowl to butter all sides. Cover and let rise in a warm place about 1 hour or until doubled in bulk. Punch down. Shape into a loaf to fit a greased 9'' x 5'' x 3'' loaf pan. Cover and let rise in a warm place about 1 hour or until doubled in bulk. Bake at 400°F for 25 to 30 minutes or until golden brown.
Yield: 1 loaf

irish soda bread

Served with generous amounts of butter, Irish soda bread disappears fast. Always let it cool before cutting. It is good toasted, too, served with your favorite marmalade.

3 cups all-purpose flour
1 teaspoon salt
1½ teaspoons baking soda
1 teaspoon sugar

2 tablespoons chilled butter or
    margarine
1¼ cups buttermilk

Lock bowl in position. Insert **steel blade**. Put all dry ingredients in bowl. Cut butter into small pieces and add to bowl. Process until well blended with flour mixture. While still processing, add buttermilk through chute, adding just enough to cause mixture to form a ball. Remove to floured surface. Shape into a ball and place in a greased 8'' round cake pan. Pat down to fit pan and cut 2 gashes on top in shape of a cross. Bake in a preheated 400°F oven 30 to 35 minutes or untill well browned. Cool on rack.
Yield: 1 loaf

muffins with variations

When the rest of the meal seems dull to you, pull a pan of hot muffins from the oven and they'll think you are a genius!

2 cups all-purpose flour	**4 tablespoons butter or margarine,**
2 tablespoons sugar	**chilled**
3 teaspoons baking powder	**1 egg**
¾ teaspoon salt	**1 cup milk**

Lock bowl in position. Insert **steel blade**. Put flour, sugar, baking powder, and salt in bowl. Cut butter into small pieces and place over flour. Process until blended. Add egg and milk through chute and process just until flour is moistened. Fill greased muffin tins ⅔ full and bake at 400°F for 20 to 25 minutes.
Yield: About 1 dozen 2'' muffins

Cheese Muffins: With **shredder disc**, grate 2 ounces American cheese in processor. Insert **steel blade** and continue mixing as above.

Cranberry Muffins: Increase sugar to 6 tablespoons. Add ¾ cup whole cranberries with milk and egg.

Blueberry Muffins: Add 1 cup blueberries with egg and milk.

ginger muffins

Serve ginger muffins with your next fruit salad luncheon.

2 cups flour	**¼ cup sugar**
3 teaspoons baking powder	**¼ cup shortening, chilled**
¾ teaspoon salt	**1 egg**
½ teaspoon ground ginger	**¼ cup molasses**
½ teaspoon cinnamon	**⅔ cup milk**
¼ teaspoon cloves	

Lock bowl in position. Insert **steel blade**. Combine flour, baking powder, salt, spices, and sugar in bowl. Cut chilled shortening into small pieces and place over flour mixture. Process until mixture is blended. Through chute add egg, molasses, and milk. Process just until all dry ingredients are moistened. Fill greased and floured muffin tins ⅔ full. Bake at 400°F for 20 to 25 minutes.
Yield: 1 dozen 2'' muffins

honey-bran yogurt muffins

These are really "some-mores," since one is never enough.

3 tablespoons shortening
½ cup honey
½ cup plain yogurt
1 egg
1 cup all-bran

1 cup whole wheat flour
1/8 teaspoon salt
¼ teaspoon baking soda
1 teaspoon baking powder
½ cup raisins

Lock bowl in position. Insert **steel blade**. Put in shortening, honey, yogurt, egg, and all-bran. Process once on MOMENTARY and let stand 5 minutes. Mix together flour, salt, soda, and baking powder. At the end of the 5 minutes add with raisins through chute. Process just until blended. Spoon batter into a dozen 2" greased and floured muffin tins. Bake at 400°F for 15 minutes. Let stand a few minutes before removing from muffin tins.
Yield: 1 dozen

wheaten bread

A recipe borrowed from the Irish, this is inclined to be heavier than white bread, but good nevertheless.

¾ cup milk
1 package active dry yeast
1 tablespoon sugar
1 cup all-purpose flour
1 cup whole wheat flour

1 cup uncooked oatmeal
1½ teaspoons salt
2 tablespoons chilled butter or
    margarine

Heat milk to lukewarm. Add yeast and sugar. Stir and let stand for 5 minutes. Lock bowl in position. Insert **steel blade**. Add flours, oatmeal, salt, and butter cut into pieces. Process 1 or 2 seconds until butter is blended with flour. Add yeast mixture through chute and process until dough forms a ball. Remove dough to a floured surface and cut into 2 pieces. Break each half into 3 or 4 pieces and press against **steel blade**. Process until dough forms a ball. Break apart and process again. Repeat with other half of dough. Combine both halves in a buttered bowl and butter dough on all sides. Cover with wax paper and a towel and let rise in a warm place until doubled in bulk. Punch down and shape into a round ball. Put into a greased 8" cake pan and let rise again until doubled in bulk, about 1½ hours. Bake at 400°F for 30 to 35 minutes. Remove from pan at once and cool on rack, covered with a towel. If desired, the hot bread may be brushed with butter.
Yield: 1 round loaf

cranberry wine bread

Cranberry wine bread is easy to make in the food processor. Bake several loaves and freeze some for future needs.

1 cup whole cranberries
2 cups all-purpose flour
1 cup sugar
1½ teaspoons baking powder
½ teaspoon baking soda
1 teaspoon salt

½ teaspoon cinnamon
¼ cup shortening at room
   temperature
½ cup uncut nuts
¾ cup white wine
1 egg

Lock bowl in position. Insert **steel blade**. Add cranberries and process 1 or 2 seconds until cranberries are coarsely chopped. Remove cranberries from bowl. Leave **steel blade** in place. Mix together dry ingredients and place in work bowl. (No need to wash it.) Add shortening and nuts and process until mixed with dry ingredients. Add wine and egg through chute. Process just until all flour is moistened. Fold in chopped cranberries. Spoon batter into a greased and floured 9'' x 5'' x 3'' loaf pan and bake at 350°F for 1 hour. Cool in pan on rack for 10 minutes. Carefully remove from pan and cool loaf on rack. When cooled, wrap in aluminum foil, and let stand overnight before cutting. Loaf will keep for several weeks under refrigeration.
Yield: 1 loaf

hush puppies

Hush puppies are a Southern treat wonderful with fried fish.

1 small onion
1½ cups yellow cornmeal
½ cup all-purpose flour
2 teaspoons baking powder

½ teaspoon salt
1 egg
¾ cup milk
Fat for frying

Peel onion and cut into 3 or 4 pieces. Lock bowl in position. Insert **steel blade**. Put in onion and process until finely chopped. Remove **steel blade** and insert **plastic blade**. To onion, add cornmeal, flour, baking powder, salt, egg, and milk. Process just until all ingredients are blended. Heat about 2 inches of fat or oil in a skillet until hot. Drop tablespoons of batter in hot fat and fry until golden brown on both sides, about 4 to 5 minutes. Serve at once with butter.
Yield: About 20

popovers

Here is a breeze of a recipe for a fabulous hot bread.

2 eggs
½ teaspoon salt
1 cup milk

1 cup all-purpose flour
1 tablespoon melted butter, cooled

Lock bowl in position. Insert **plastic blade**. Put all ingredients into bowl. Process a few seconds until smooth. Scrape down sides of processor once. Pour batter into 8 well-greased pyrex custard cups. Place on a cookie sheet and bake at 425°F for 40 minutes. Serve at once.
Note: Although not absolutely necessary, some directions suggest that the popovers should be pricked with a fork just before they are ready to come from the oven, to allow steam to escape. It is worth remembering that if the popovers are done before the dinner is ready, leave them in the oven, heat off, door slightly ajar. This makes for a little drier popover, but it is still a super taste.
Yield: 8 popovers

Nut Popovers: Chop 1 cup pecans or almonds very fine with **steel blade** and incorporate in batter mixed with **plastic blade**.

Cheese Popovers: Lock bowl in place. Insert **shredder disc**. Grate 4 ounces chilled sharp Cheddar cheese. Remove **shredder disc**, insert **plastic disc**, and proceed as directed.

blueberry coffee cake

Whether served warm or cold, this cake is yummy.

2 cups all-purpose flour
2 teaspoons baking powder
½ teaspoon baking soda
½ cup sugar

4 tablespoons chilled butter or
    margarine
1 egg
¾ cup plain yogurt
1 cup blueberries

Lock bowl in position. Insert **steel blade**. Add dry ingredients. Cut butter into small pieces and place over flour mixture. Process to blend. Add egg and yogurt through chute and process until all flour is moistened. Add blueberries and process on MOMENTARY. Spoon batter into a greased and floured 8'' x 8'' x 2'' pan. Bake at 375°F 30 to 35 minutes. Cut into squares to serve.
Yield: 9 squares

hurry-up pancakes

For a quick treat on a cold morning, serve hot griddle cakes with butter and syrup.

1 egg
1¼ cups milk
2 tablespoons vegetable oil

2 tablespoons dark corn syrup
1 cup pancake mix

Lock bowl in position. Insert **plastic blade**. Add all ingredients to bowl. Process until batter is smooth. For each pancake, spoon about 2 tablespoons batter onto hot griddle. When bubbles begin to break, turn to cook other side.
Yield: About 1 dozen pancakes

dumplings for stew

When it's a cold, wintry day and you want to add something special to a lamb stew, stewed chicken, or a pork stew made from leftover roast pork, cook dumplings on top of the stew the last 15 minutes and wait for the raves.

Cheese Dumplings

2 ounces sharp Cheddar cheese
1½ cups all-purpose flour
2 teaspoons baking powder
½ teaspoon salt

2 tablespoons chilled butter or margarine
½ to ¾ cup milk

Lock bowl in position. Insert **steel blade**. Cut cheese into cubes and process until finely chopped. Add flour, baking powder, and salt. Cut butter into pieces and distribute over flour. Process until butter is blended. Continue processing and add milk through chute until a ball forms. Drop by spoonsful on top of stew. (Dip spoon in stew between each spoonful for easy release.) Cover and cook 15 minutes.
Yield: 4 servings

Plain Dumplings: Omit cheese.

Herbed Dumplings: Add 7 or 8 sprigs parsley and 5 or 6 cut-up chives to flour mixture.

Sage Dumplings: Add ½ teaspoon dried sage to flour mixture.

noodles

Once upon a time, noodles were made at home. If you're old enough, you may remember your mother placing a broom across the backs of two chairs, covering the broom handle with a clean towel, and hanging the noodles over that to dry.

With the advent of the food processor, homemade noodles are once again being made and enjoyed by the space-age generation.

1 cup all-purpose flour
¼ teaspoon salt

1 egg yolk
3 to 4 tablespoons water

Lock bowl in position. Insert **steel blade**. Add flour, salt, and egg yolk to bowl. Process until egg yolk is blended into flour and while processor is running add water, 1 tablespoon at a time until dough forms a ball on blades. Remove dough to a floured board. Cut in half and cut each half into 3 or 4 pieces and place on edge of blade. Process until dough more or less forms a ball and repeat once more. Repeat with other half of dough. Combine both pieces and cover loosely with wax paper or plastic wrap and let rest 30 minutes. With a well-floured rolling pin, and on a well-floured board, roll a half or a third of dough as thinly as possible into a rectangle about 3'' wide. If the dough is well floured, it can be folded over to cut several thicknesses at once to the desired width. Then separate strands and lay out on a cake rack or wax paper to dry. When dry, noodles can be cooked in boiling water for about 10 minutes or used in any recipe calling for noodles.
Yield: About 8 ounces of noodles

Pastries

Such a variety of foods turn up under the name of pastry, even though we often think of pies first in the pastry category, that a sampling of recipes is included in this chapter. The one thing you will learn is that the processor is invaluable in making pie crusts of all kinds, cream puffs, or pastry in any of its variations.

pastry

Quick as a wink, the pastry is ready.

⅔ cup shortening
2 cups all-purpose flour

½ teaspoon salt
¼ cup ice water

Chill shortening and cut into small pieces. Lock bowl in position. Insert **steel blade**. Put in flour, salt, and shortening. Process until mixture is texture of corn-meal. Add water through chute while continuing to process. Process just until a ball forms around blade. Chill about ½ hour before rolling dough. (If dough is chilled a longer time, allow to stand at room temperature for a few minutes before rolling.) Bake shells in a preheated 425°F oven 10 to 12 minutes.
Yield: Either a 9'' or 10'' two-crust pie or two 9'' or 10'' baked pie shells

graham cracker pie crust

This is a basic graham cracker crust. Use it for cream or gelatin fillings.

17 single graham crackers
½ cup brown sugar

½ cup butter or margarine, melted

Lock bowl in position. Insert **steel blade**. Break up graham crackers and process to medium-fine crumbs. Add sugar and margarine and process just until blended. Pat into 9'' pie plate. Chill well. If desired, save 2 tablespoons crumbs to sprinkle on top of pie.
Yield: 1 9'' crust

open-face apple-raisin pie

An easy-as-pie recipe, so good you will serve it often.

½ **lemon**
1 **cup sugar**
1 **egg**
5 **medium cooking apples**

2 **tablespoons soft butter or margarine**
½ **cup raisins**
1 **unbaked 9" pie shell (see page 118)**

Wash lemon and cut in half crosswise to remove seeds. Cut again into several pieces. Lock bowl in position and insert **steel blade**. Add lemon, sugar, and egg and process until lemon is chopped fine. Remove **steel blade**. Insert **shredder disc**. Peel apples, cut into quarters, and remove core. Pack into chute and process to shred. If work bowl becomes too full, remove contents to another bowl until remaining apples are shredded. Carefully mix processed lemon mixture and apples with butter and raisins. Spoon into unbaked pie shell and bake at 350°F for 40 to 45 minutes or until filling is set. Serve warm or cold.
Yield: 1 9'' pie

pineapple pie

This pie, made from fresh, grated pineapple would take hours without the food processor. Now you can effortlessly produce this pie luxuriously reminiscent of South Sea islands.

1 **ripe pineapple**
2 **tablespoons flour**
½ **cup sugar**
1 **egg**

½ **teaspoon cinnamon**
¼ **teaspoon nutmeg**
2 **tablespoons butter**
1 **recipe for pastry (see page 118)**

Cut off top of pineapple and cut into fourths lengthwise. Cut out core and remove outer peel. Cut pieces to fit chute. Lock bowl in position. Insert **shredder disc**. Feed pineapple into chute until it is all grated. There should be about 2 cups. Put pineapple in a bowl and add flour, sugar, egg, spices, and butter. Mix well. Roll out half of pastry and fit into a 9'' pie plate. Add filling. Roll out remaining pastry and cover pie, sealing edges. Cut several slits in top to vent steam. Bake at 425°F for 50 to 60 minutes.
Yield: 1 9'' pie

leslie's pumpkin pie

Here is a gentle combination of flavors with an old favorite—pumpkin.

3 tablespoons pecans
3 tablespoons brown sugar
¾ cup undiluted evaporated milk
Thin yellow peel from 1 orange
½ cup orange juice
2 eggs

1 cup canned pumpkin
⅔ cup honey
1/8 teaspoon nutmeg
½ teaspoon cinnamon
1/8 teaspoon ginger
1 unbaked 9" pie shell (see page 118)

Lock bowl in position. Insert **steel blade**. Process pecans until medium-fine. Remove from bowl and mix with brown sugar. Reserve.

Combine remaining ingredients except pie shell and process with **steel blade** until blended and orange peel chopped fine, pushing down from sides of bowl once. Pour into unbaked pie shell and bake at 425°F for 40 minutes or until set in center. Five minutes before pie is removed from oven, sprinkle top with pecan-sugar mixture.

Yield: 1 9" pie

english apple pie

Served warm with a scoop of butter pecan ice cream, this is a real dessert.

6 to 8 cooking apples, depending
    on size
¾ cup granulated sugar
½ teaspoon cinnamon
½ teaspoon nutmeg

1 cup all-purpose flour
½ cup brown sugar
Dash salt
½ cup butter or margarine, chilled

Peel and core apples and cut into quarters. Lock bowl in position. Insert **slicer disc**. Cut apple quarters to fit chute, if necessary, and slice. As work bowl becomes full, place apples in a buttered 9" pie plate. When all apples are sliced, pie plate should be heaping. Mix granulated sugar with spices and pour over apples.

Remove **slicer disc** and insert **steel blade**. Put flour, sugar, and salt in bowl and cut butter into it in small pieces. Process just until blended. Carefully spoon over apples in pie plate. Bake at 425°F in a preheated oven for about 40 minutes or until apples are tender.

Yield: 6 servings

napoleons

Dare to make these. They look more complicated to make than they are.

Pastry

½ recipe basic pastry (see page 118)

Roll pastry into a 12'' square. Cut into 3 equal strips, 4'' x 12'' each. Transfer to a baking sheet and prick well with fork. Bake in a preheated oven at 425°F about 12 minutes or until lightly browned. Cool.

Cream Filling

1 package (4-serving size) vanilla pudding and pie filling
1 cup milk

½ cup frozen whipped non-dairy topping, defrosted

Prepare pudding and pie filling mix as directed on package, using only 1 cup milk. Cover surface of cooked filling with wax paper. Chill. Lock bowl in position. Insert **plastic blade**. Process filling until light and smooth. Add topping and process until blended. Spread 2 of the cooled pastry strips with filling. Stack, filling side up.

Icing

¾ cup confectioners' sugar
1½ to 2 tablespoons water
1½ to 2 teaspoons water

1 square (1 ounce) unsweetened chocolate, melted

Mix confectioners' sugar with 1½ to 2 tablespoons water and spread on third strip of pastry carefully, so it does not drip over edges. Gradually blend 1½ to 2 teaspoons water into melted chocolate until thin enough to pour. Then drizzle from a spoon into thin lines the length of the frosted pastry about ½'' apart. Draw a sharp knife across lines, alternating from side to side, to give a rippled effect. Place on top of stacked layers. Chill about 2 hours. Cut with a sharp knife and quick cutting strokes into a half dozen 2'' pieces.
Yield: 6 servings

quiche

The quiche has become almost what anyone wants to make it. This is a version of the original quiche served in a Swiss restaurant in New York City—a lightly seasoned Swiss cheese pie. The food processor lightens the work immeasurably.

8 ounces Swiss cheese
1 tablespoon flour
3 eggs
1 cup cream
½ teaspoon salt

Fresh ground pepper to taste
6 slices bacon
1 unbaked 9" pie shell (see page 118)
Paprika

Lock bowl in position. Insert **shredder disc**. Cut cheese to fit disc and grate. Remove **shredder disc** and insert **plastic blade**. Add flour, eggs, cream, salt, and pepper. Process to blend. Pan fry bacon until crisp. Drain on absorbent paper and crumble. Put on bottom of pie shell. Pour cheese mixture over. Sprinkle with paprika. Bake at 375°F for about 40 minutes or until custard is set. Cut in wedges to serve.
Yield: 1 9" quiche

cheese sticks

If a yellow Cheddar is used, these cheese sticks have a lovely color. Serve with soup, salad, or cocktails.

4 ounces sharp Cheddar cheese
1 cup all-purpose flour
½ teaspoon celery salt
¼ teaspoon dry mustard

5 tablespoons butter or margarine, chilled
1 to 3 tablespoons ice water

Cut cheese into cubes. Lock bowl in position. Insert **steel blade**. Process cheese until fine. Remove half of cheese from bowl and reserve. Add flour, seasonings, and butter, cut into small pieces, to cheese still in bowl. Add water through chute and process until a ball is formed.

Roll out on a well-floured pastry cloth into a 12" x 6" rectangle. Sprinkle with half of the reserved cheese. Fold half pastry over cheese and roll again. Sprinkle with remaining cheese, fold over and roll out again.

Divide pastry in half and roll half into a 12" x 6" rectangle. With a pastry cutter or a knife, cut into strips 6" long and ½" wide. Transfer to baking sheet and bake at 350°F for 12 to 15 minutes. Repeat with other half of pastry.
Yield: 4½ to 5 dozen

Desserts, Cakes, and Cookies

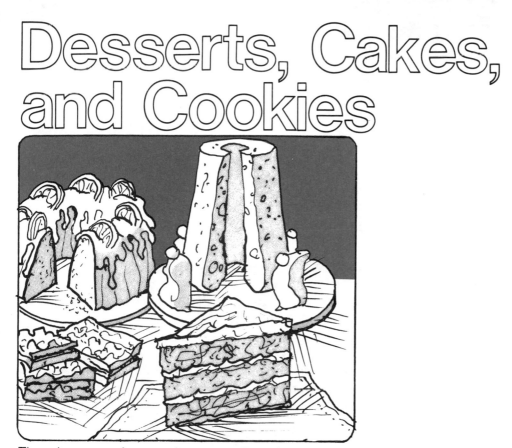

The pleasure of preparing appealing desserts in a fraction of the time is yours with the processor. Creaming, chopping, mixing, blending—all are at hand with the processor doing the work.

baba au rhum

A sophisticated dessert everyone loves, "baba" means "old woman" in some Slavic countries. Here it's a rich cake soaked in rum-and-sugar syrup.

½ cup milk
1 package active dry yeast
1 tablespoon sugar
2 cups all-purpose flour
½ cup sugar
½ teaspoon salt

Thin yellow rind from 1 lemon
½ cup butter or margarine, chilled
3 eggs
Orange Rum Syrup
Apricot jam

Heat milk to lukewarm and mix with yeast, 1 tablespoon sugar, and ½ cup of the flour. Cover and let stand 1 hour in a warm place.

Lock bowl in position. Insert **steel blade**. Put remaining flour, ½ cup sugar, salt, and lemon rind in bowl. Cut butter into small pieces and place over flour. Process until mixture resembles cornmeal. Through chute, add eggs and yeast mixture. Process just to blend.

Pour batter into greased and floured 8-cup Turk's-head mold, ring mold, or bundt cake pan. Cover with greased wax paper and let rise in a warm place until doubled in bulk. Bake at 350°F for 40 to 50 minutes. Remove from pan to cake rack and cool. Put cooled cake on a serving platter and spoon orange rum syrup over cake. Spread with apricot jam to glaze.
Yield: 1 baba

Orange Rum Syrup: Combine ½ cup sugar with ¼ cup water and boil 1 minute. Cool and add ½ cup each orange juice and light rum.

lacey cookies

Here are lovely, crisp cookies to serve with tea.

1 cup blanched almonds
½ cup sugar
½ cup butter

1 tablespoon flour
2 tablespoons milk

Lock bowl in position. Insert **steel blade**. Process nuts, a half cup at a time, until very finely ground. Combine with remaining ingredients in a small saucepan and stir and blend over moderate heat until butter is melted. Drop by teaspoonfuls on a greased and floured baking sheet. Bake in a preheated 350°F oven 6 to 8 minutes. Remove carefully with a spatula to a rack to cool.
Yield: About 2 dozen cookies

profiteroles au chocolat

These tiny cream puffs, filled with a cream filling or ice cream, and served with hot chocolate sauce or other sauce of your choice, make a popular dessert.

Cream Puffs

¾ cup boiling water	¾ cup flour
1/8 teaspoon salt	3 eggs
6 tablespoons butter	

Combine boiling water, salt, and butter in saucepan. Add flour all at once and cook and stir over moderate heat until the mixture forms a ball and leaves the sides of the pan. Remove from heat and let cool 5 minutes. Lock bowl in position. Insert **steel blade**. Turn flour mixture into bowl. Begin processing and add eggs one at a time through chute. Process well between each egg. Scrape mixture from sides of bowl. When all eggs have been added, the dough should be firm enough to hold its shape when dropped from spoon onto ungreased baking sheet. Bake at 425°F for 30 minutes or until lightly browned and crisp. Cool.

     Split cooled cream puffs and fill with the cream filling used for Napoleons found on page 121 or ice cream.
Yield: 2 dozen small puffs

Chocolate Sauce

4 squares (4 ounces) unsweetened chocolate	1 tablespoon corn syrup
2 tablespoons cornstarch dissolved in	Dash salt
	1 tablespoon butter or margarine softened
2 cups water	1½ teaspoons vanilla extract
1 cup sugar	

Lock bowl in position. Insert **plastic blade**. Melt chocolate and combine with remaining ingredients in work bowl. Process until smooth. Pour into a saucepan and cook and stir until mixture boils and is thickened. Serve hot over filled cream puffs.
Yield: About 2 cups

almond paste coconut macaroons

Now you can make these dainty confections yourself.

Unsweetened Almond Paste

1¼ cups blanched almonds
2 to 3 tablespoons water

½ teaspoon almond extract

Lock bowl in position and insert **steel blade**. Place almonds in bowl and process until very finely ground. Stop processor and push ground almonds from side of bowl several times. Add water and almond extract through the chute and process until mixture forms a ball. If not to be used at once, cover tightly and store in refrigerator.
Yield: 1 cup

Macaroons

1 cup unsweetened almond paste
4 egg whites
¾ cup sugar
1½ tablespoons all-purpose flour

¼ teaspoon salt
1 cup chopped fresh coconut
(see page 128)

Lock bowl in position and insert **steel blade**. Add all ingredients and process until mixture is blended. With 2 teaspoons, make thick macaroons about the size of a quarter on a well-greased cookie sheet. Bake at 300°F for 30 minutes or until lightly browned. Remove from cookie sheet with spatula and cool on cake rack. Store in a covered container.
Yield: About 3 dozen

quickie lemon ice cream

Your processor is a great way to get a new flavor of ice cream.

1 lemon
½ cup sugar

1 quart vanilla ice cream

Wash lemon and cut into quarters lengthwise. Cut a V through center of each piece and remove seeds. Cut quarters in half again. Lock bowl in position. Insert **steel blade**. Process lemon with sugar until finely chopped. If sugar does not dissolve completely, remove lemon-sugar mixture from work bowl and put into dish. Place dish over hot water, stirring until sugar dissolves. Cool. Soften vanilla ice cream and mix lemon into it. Refreeze.
Yield: 4 to 6 servings

chocolate sour cream cake

This cake made with oat flour is a delight. The cake has a different texture because of the oat flour and a divine flavor.

2½ cups uncooked oatmeal
1 cup water
½ cup butter or margarine
2 squares (2 ounces) unsweetened
      chocolate
1½ cups sugar

½ cup all-purpose flour
1 teaspoon baking soda
½ teaspoon salt
2 eggs
½ cup dairy sour cream

Lock bowl in position. Insert **steel blade**. Put oatmeal in work bowl and process until a fine flour is formed. There should be 2 cups.
      Combine water, butter, and chocolate in a saucepan and bring to a boil. Remove from heat and cool. Add chocolate mixture and remaining ingredients to oat flour and process just until blended, pushing down from sides with spatula once. Pour batter into a greased and floured 13" x 9" baking pan. Bake in a pre-heated 375°F oven 30 to 35 minutes or until toothpick inserted in center comes out clean. Cool on rack.
Yield: 15 squares

Frosting: Melt together 1 square (1 ounce) unsweetened chocolate and 1 teaspoon butter or margarine in a heavy small saucepan. Stir in 1 cup confectioners' sugar and 5 teaspoons hot water, a spoon at a time, until frosting can be drizzled over cooled cake. Sprinkle with ¼ cup chopped nuts.

fresh coconut snow

A rich, yet light dessert made easy now that the grated fresh coconut is prepared in the food processor. *

2 envelopes unflavored gelatin
½ cup cold water
2 cups light cream
1 cup sugar
1/8 teaspoon salt

1 teaspoon almond extract
2 cups whipping cream
2 cups grated fresh coconut
Sugared green grapes
Chocolate sauce, if desired

Soften gelatin in cold water. Heat light cream to boiling point. Add gelatin, sugar, salt, and almond extract. Cool until mixture begins to thicken. Whip cream and fold along with coconut into chilled mixture. Spoon into a 6- to 7-cup mold and chill until firm. Unmold on platter. Garnish with sugared green grapes. (Dip small bunches of grapes in slightly beaten egg white and then in granulated sugar. Let stand until dry.) If desired, serve with chocolate sauce (see page 125).
Yield: 6 to 8 servings

* See recipe for ambrosia below for directions for preparing coconut.

ambrosia

This is a Southern dessert, always served at Christmas. Sometimes white grapes are added.

1 fresh coconut
4 cups orange sections

¾ cup sugar

Break eye of coconut and pour out milk. Break coconut open with hammer. Put pieces in a warm oven for 5 to 10 minutes and hard shell will come off easily. Peel off remaining dark skin with a sharp knife. Cut coconut to fit chute. Lock bowl in position. Insert **shredder disc** and grate coconut. Measure 1½ cups. If there is more than 1½ cups, it can be stored in a covered container in the refrigerator for future use.

Choose your prettiest serving bowl (about 6-cup capacity) and layer coconut and oranges in bowl. Sprinkle sugar on each layer, ending with coconut. Cover bowl with plastic wrap and chill thoroughly.
Yield: About 8 servings

jam pudding

A bountiful dessert to finish off a light meal.

½ cup butter or margarine
1 cup sugar
3 eggs
1 cup all-purpose flour
1 teaspoon cinnamon
½ teaspoon nutmeg

¼ teaspoon salt
1 teaspoon baking soda
1 cup cherry jam
½ cup plain yogurt
Whipped topping

Lock bowl in position. Insert **steel blade**. Put butter, sugar, and eggs in bowl and process until blended and fluffy. Mix flour with dry ingredients. Add 4 tablespoons of this mixture and jam and process to blend. Add remaining flour and yogurt and blend. Bake in a greased and floured 9'' x 9'' x 2'' pan at 350°F for 30 to 35 minutes. Serve warm, cut in squares, with whipped topping.
Yield: 9 squares

blintzes

Dessert blintzes are folded in from opposite sides and then rolled so they are like little packages. Two or three are a serving. Make them bigger for a light main course dish. Serve with chilled sour cream.

1 recipe crepes (see page 71)
2 cups small curd cottage cheese
1 egg yolk
½ teaspoon salt
1 tablespoon soft butter

2 tablespoons sugar
2 teaspoons lemon juice
2 tablespoons raisins, plumped
    in hot water, drained
Dairy sour cream

Prepare crepes as directed. Lock bowl in position. Insert **steel blade**. Add filling ingredients, except sour cream. Process until blended and smooth. Put 1 tablespoon of filling on light side of each crepe. Turn opposite sides in and roll up like a jelly roll. Place seam side down in a buttered flat baking dish and bake at 425°F for about 10 minutes or until heated through.
Yield: 16 blintzes

lemony cottage cheese torte

This cake is a little lower calorically than a regular cheese cake and still delicious.

Crust

3 slices dry bread	2 tablespoons sugar
4 tablespoons butter, chilled	½ teaspoon cinnamon

Lock bowl in position. Insert **steel blade**. Break bread into pieces and put into bowl. Process to coarse crumbs. Cut butter into pieces and add with sugar and cinnamon to crumbs. Process until blended. Pat mixture firmly into the bottom of a greased 9" layer-cake pan.

Filling

Yellow peel from 1 lemon	2 tablespoons lemon juice
2 cups large or small curd cottage	⅔ cup sugar
cheese	¼ teaspoon salt
½ cup light cream	3 tablespoons flour
2 eggs	

Lock bowl in position. Insert **steel blade**. Add lemon peel and cottage cheese and process until smooth. Add remaining ingredients through chute and process just to blend. Pour into crust-lined pan. Bake at 325°F for about 1 hour or until set in center. Cool to cut.
Yield: 1 9" torte

brandy frappe

This is an easy dessert that's both glamorous and rich. Serve in chilled glasses with a spoon and straws

1 quart coffee ice cream	4 tablespoons chocolate syrup
1 cup brandy	

Lock bowl in position. Insert **steel blade**. Cut ice cream into pieces and process half at a time with half the brandy and chocolate syrup until just blended. Repeat.
Yield: 4 servings

peanut cookies

Good as a snack with milk, these are a favorite with kids of all ages.

1 cup unsalted roasted peanuts
½ cup shortening
½ cup granulated sugar
½ cup brown sugar, firmly packed
½ teaspoon salt
2 tablespoons milk

1 egg
1 teaspoon vanilla
1¼ cups all-purpose flour
¾ teaspoon baking soda
½ teaspoon baking powder

Lock bowl in position. Insert **steel blade**. Process peanuts until they are about half their original size. Add remaining ingredients and process until blended. Push down from sides with spatula once. Chill batter about 30 minutes. Form into small balls and put on ungreased cookie sheets. Dip the tines of a fork in water and push balls flat with fork, leaving a criss-cross mark on top of cookies. Bake at 375°F for 10 minutes.
Yield: 4 dozen

chocolate nut bars

Quick and good. Cut into large squares and serve a la mode with chocolate sauce or cut small squares for cookie-bars.

2¼ cups all-purpose flour
1 teaspoon baking soda
½ teaspoon salt
¾ cup granulated sugar
¾ cup granulated brown sugar

½ cup uncut walnuts
1 stick butter or margarine, chilled
2 eggs
2 tablespoons water
1 teaspoon vanilla extract
1 cup semi-sweet chocolate morsels

Mix together flour, soda, salt, sugars, and nuts. Lock bowl in position. Insert **steel blade**. Empty dry ingredients into work bowl. Cut butter into small pieces and arrange over dry ingredients. Process until butter is well blended. Add eggs, water and vanilla through chute and process just to blend. Add chocolate morsels through chute and blend 1 or 2 seconds. Spread batter into a greased 15"×10"×1" baking pan. Bake at 375°F for 20 to 25 minutes. Cool and cut into squares. **Yield:** 15 squares.

double apple jelly

Here is a good fall or winter dessert.

1 lemon
2 envelopes unflavored gelatin
1½ cups water
2 cups sweet cider

1 cup sugar
2 eating apples
Dairy sour cream

Lock bowl into position. Insert **steel blade**. Cut lemon lengthwise into quarters. Remove any seeds, white center, and cut off heavy ends. Process until lemon is finely chopped. Combine gelatin with water to soften. Add cider, sugar, and lemon and bring to a boil. Strain.

Lock bowl in position. Insert **steel blade**. Peel and core apples and process to chop coarsely. Add to strained cider mixture. Chill until mixture begins to become firm. Pour into a 6-cup ring mold and chill until firm. To serve, unmold on platter and fill center with dairy sour cream.

Yield: 6 servings

rhubarb orange sauce

This taste of spring is a light finale for a meal.

1 pound fresh rhubarb
1 navel orange
¼ cup water

6 tablespoons sugar
¼ cup raisins, if desired

Wash rhubarb and trim off ends. Cut in lengths to fit chute. Wash orange, cut off stem end and cut into quarters and remove seeds, if any.

Lock bowl in position. Insert **French cutter disc**. Pack chute with rhubarb standing upright. Process, using light pressure with pusher. Replace **French cutter** with **slicer disc**. Pack orange pieces into chute to be cut crosswise. Process.

Combine rhubarb and oranges with remaining ingredients in a saucepan. Bring to a boil and simmer about 5 minutes. Chill to serve.

Yield: 4 to 6 servings

Beverages

Mix up your own concoctions. Here are a few for a start. Remember, the work bowl has a 4-cup capacity, so if you're thinking big, do the processing in several batches.

fruit cooler

This summer beverage can become a quick change artist for finicky appetites.

1 cup chilled fruit juice	**Sugar**
Lemon juice	**1 or 2 servings vanilla ice cream**

Lock bowl in position. Insert **plastic blade**. Combine fruit juice, lemon juice, sugar, and ice cream and process 1 or 2 seconds just to blend.
Yield: 1 serving

Apricot Cooler

1 cup chilled apricot nectar	**1 tablespoon sugar**
2 teaspoons lemon juice	**Large serving vanilla ice cream**

Pineapple Cooler

1 cup chilled pineapple juice	**2 large servings vanilla ice cream**
1 tablespoon lemon juice	

Grape Cooler

1 cup chilled grape juice	**1 large serving vanilla ice cream**
1 tablespoon sugar	

Lemon Cooler

1 cup ice water	**¼ cup sugar**
¼ cup lemon juice	**1 large serving vanilla ice cream**

summer cooler

1 cup chilled orange juice   **1 cup chilled watermelon, diced**
1 tablespoon lemon juice

Lock bowl in position. Insert **steel blade**. Combine all ingredients in bowl. Process until blended. Serve over ice cubes.
Yield: 2 servings

pineapple-grape ade

1 tablespoon instant tea   **1 tablespoon lemon juice**
    with lemon   **2 cups grape juice**
1 cup ice water   **1 cup pineapple juice**
4 slices pineapple

Lock bowl in position. Insert **steel blade**. Combine tea, ice water, and pineapple slices which have been cut up. Process until blended. Add to remaining ingredients and serve over ice.
Yield: 1½ quarts

carrot-pineapple picker-upper

1 cup pineapple juice   **1 carrot, peeled, cut into 1" pieces**
1 tablespoon lemon juice

Lock bowl in position. Insert **steel blade**. Combine ingredients in bowl and process until smooth. Serve over ice cubes.
Yield: 1 serving

lemon syrup

This base for fresh lemonade can be kept in your refrigerator.

6 lemons   **½ cup water**
1½ cups sugar

Cut the thin yellow peel from the lemon with a paring knife. Place the peel and sugar in the processor bowl with the **steel blade** in place. Process until the peel is finely chopped. Remove and discard the outer white membrane from the lemons. Quarter and seed the lemons. Add lemons and water to peel and sugar mixture. Process until smooth. Strain if desired. Pour into covered container and chill. To make lemonade, combine ¼ cup of the syrup, ¾ cup of water, and several ice cubes for 1 8-ounce serving.
Yield: 2 cups lemon syrup

lime syrup

Use this syrup for limeade or other beverages.

3 medium to large limes   **¼ cup water**
¾ cup sugar

Cut a substantial slice off each end of limes and cut into eight pieces. Remove seeds. Lock bowl in position. Insert **steel blade**. Add limes and sugar and process until fine. Add water and continue processing to blend, pushing down from sides of bowl several times. Strain into jar. Cover. Refrigerate. Use to make limeade, ¼ to ½ cup water and ice cubes, or to flavor such drinks as Daiquiris, rum and cola, or gin and tonic.
Yield: 1 cup

chocolate peanut milk

1 cup chilled milk
½ cup roasted, hulled peanuts

¼ cup chocolate syrup

Lock bowl in position. Insert **steel blade**. Process until smooth.
Yield: 2 servings

molasses milk shake

Try this for a refreshing change.

Thin yellow peel from ¼ lemon
2 tablespoons light molasses
2 tablespoons lemon juice

1 teaspoon sugar
1 cup chilled milk
Large serving vanilla ice cream

Lock bowl in position. Insert **steel blade**. Add lemon peel, molasses, lemon juice, sugar, and milk and process to blend and chop lemon. Add vanilla ice cream and process on MOMENTARY.
Yield: 1 serving

chocolate milk shake

This is a traditional favorite with all members of the family.

¾ cup cold milk
2 tablespoons chocolate syrup

**2 scoops vanilla or chocolate
    ice cream**

Lock bowl in position and insert **plastic blade**. Add chocolate syrup and ice cream. Lock cover in place and while using MOMENTARY setting, add milk through chute to mix. Pour in glass to serve.
Yield: 1 serving

prune fluff

1 cup soaked prunes, pitted
1 cup vanilla ice cream
2 tablespoons molasses

1/8 teaspoon cinnamon
2 cups chilled milk

Cover prunes with water and soak overnight in the refrigerator. When ready for use, drain, remove pits, and cut prunes into pieces. Lock bowl in position. Insert **steel blade**. Combine all ingredients in bowl and process just to blend.
Yield: 2 to 3 servings

eggnog with sherry

Try this traditional beverage whenever you are in a holiday mood.

¼ cup chilled cognac
¼ cup chilled Bacardi rum
5 egg yolks
2 tablespoons sugar
Dash cinnamon

Dash nutmeg
1 cup chilled dry sherry wine
1½ cups chilled milk
½ cup heavy cream, whipped

Lock bowl in position. Insert **plastic blade**. Put cognac, rum, egg yolks, sugar, and spices in bowl and process until blended and eggs are frothy. Add sherry and half of milk through chute while processing. Put into container and add remaining milk. Chill well. When ready to serve, fold in whipped cream. Sprinkle with additional nutmeg.
Yield: 1 quart

Sandwich Fillings

The food processor really shines when it comes to making sandwich fillings. A little leftover beef, pork, chicken, lamb, or fish can be quickly turned into filling that converts it from leftover to planned for.

Not enough meat? Add a few nuts to stretch the protein and give a bit of crunch. Think of foods that go well together and chop up some apple or some bean sprouts with cold roast pork. Vary the bread—that helps vary the sandwich.

Grating cheese is such an easy job that you can almost choose any number of cheeses for sandwich fillings.

If you make lunch-box sandwiches, don't put leaf lettuce in the sandwiches—use chopped, crisp iceberg lettuce instead.

Heat-seal some water in small freezer-plastic bags and freeze them. Be sure to leave a little air space for expansion as the water freezes to ice. If you make 2 or 3, 1 can be in the lunch-box to keep things cold, and 2 in the freezer ready for use.

But cold sandwiches are only the beginning. We've included some hot sandwiches that are meal size.

beef on english muffins

This tasty combination is easy to make. The juices from the beef go into the muffin.

1 pound boneless beef chuck
½ teaspoon salt
Fresh ground pepper to taste

1 teaspoon Worcestershire sauce
4 English muffins
Softened butter

Cut beef into 1'' cubes and sprinkle with seasoning. Lock bowl into position. Insert **steel blade**. Process meat 1 cup at a time until finely chopped, removing to a bowl as processed. Split English muffins and butter. Spread seasoned beef on each half. Broil 3'' from source of heat until meat is cooked.
Yield: 4 servings

Cheese Muffins: When beef is almost done, sprinkle top with grated cheese and continue broiling to melt and brown cheese.

Surprise Muffins: Put a thin slice of tomato on muffin before adding beef.

Onion Muffins: Process a small onion, peeled and cut into pieces, with beef.

beef spread

Leftovers do become plan-overs and here is a good example of a basic recipe. You can add your own favorite seasoning such as chili sauce or Worcestershire sauce.

1 cup leftover cooked beef
1 rib celery
1 small onion
¼ cup mayonnaise

1 teaspoon prepared mustard
1 teaspoon grated horseradish
Salt and pepper to taste

Cut beef into 1'' to 2'' cubes. Wash celery and cut into 1'' pieces. Cut up onion. Lock bowl in position. Insert **steel blade**. Add all ingredients and process for a few seconds until chopped to the proper consistency for a sandwich spread. Will keep several days under refrigeration.
Yield: 1 to 1¼ cups

peanut butter

The addition of oil will make a softer peanut butter. Note that butters may be made from any nuts by following these directions.

1 cup roasted, shelled, blanched peanuts

1 tablespoon salad oil, if desired
Salt to taste, about ¼ teaspoon

Lock bowl in position. Insert **steel blade**. Place peanuts in bowl. Process until nuts form a butter of the desired consistency and texture. Add oil and salt and process long enough to blend. Cover and refrigerate.
Yield: About ¾ cup

peanut veggie spread

This spread is flavorful and would make a good open-faced sandwich with several slices of crisp bacon criss-crossed on top.

1 cup roasted, shelled, blanched peanuts
1 medium tomato
1 rib celery
1 tablespoon vinegar
1 tablespoon mayonnaise

1 teaspoon prepared mustard
½ teaspoon Worcestershire sauce
¼ teaspoon salt
Dash Tabasco sauce
1 hard-cooked egg, peeled

Lock bowl in position. Insert **steel blade**. Process peanuts until partially chopped. Meanwhile, remove stem end of tomato and cut tomato into eighths. Wash celery and cut into 1'' pieces. Add tomato, celery, and seasonings to peanuts and continue processing until mixture is blended and will spread. Cut egg into fourths and put through chute. Process on MOMENTARY. This makes a "crunchy" spread. If you prefer it smooth, run processor until the peanut butter is smooth. Then add remaining ingredients and blend. Scrape down sides of bowl with a spatula as needed.
Yield: 1½ cups

peanut butter chili spread

With such a combination of popular flavors, this delightful spread should be a hit.

1 cup roasted, shelled, blanched peanuts
⅓ cup chili sauce

2 tablespoons prepared mustard
2 tablespoons pickle relish
1 teaspoon onion salt

Lock bowl in position. Insert **steel blade**. Add peanuts and process until partially chopped. Add remaining ingredients and process until blended and will spread. This makes a "crunchy" spread. If you prefer it smooth, run processor until the peanut butter is smooth. Then add remaining ingredients and blend. Scrape down sides of bowl with spatula as needed.
Yield: 1 cup

peanutty ham

Here is another quickie, popular with the young set.

½ cup salted, blanched peanuts
1 can (4½ ounces) deviled ham
1 tablespoon catsup

6 slices bread
Butter

Lock bowl in position. Insert **steel blade**. Add peanuts and process until medium-fine. Add deviled ham and catsup and process to blend. Toast bread and butter lightly. Spread half of slices with filling and top with remaining bread.
Yield: 3 sandwiches

lamb special sandwich filling

This cold lamb spread will be eaten with relish—even by those people who think they don't like cold lamb.

2 cups cooked lamb, cubed, all
        fat removed
½ cup chutney

4 tablespoons mayonnaise
Salt and fresh ground pepper

Lock bowl in position. Insert **steel blade**. Add all ingredients and process until blended. Use as a spread for sandwiches.
Yield: 1½ cups

super lamb patties

Try this special way to serve lamb on a bun.

2 pounds boneless lamb
2 ounces Parmesan cheese
¼ cup Worcestershire sauce
8 to 10 sprigs parsley
3 sprigs fresh mint or 1 teaspoon
        dried mint flakes

2 garlic cloves, peeled
¾ teaspoon salt
3 tablespoons butter or margarine
6 hamburger buns, split and toasted
Chili sauce
Mint jelly

Remove all fat from lamb and cut into cubes. Lock bowl in position. Insert **steel blade**. Process lamb, 1 cup at a time, until finely chopped, removing to a large bowl after each processing. Cut Parmesan cheese into cubes and add with Worcestershire, parsley, mint, garlic, and salt to processor bowl. Process until well blended, pushing down from side of bowl once. Mix with chopped lamb. Shape into 6 patties. Heat butter in skillet and cook lamb patties until browned, turning to cook both sides. Serve on toasted buns with chili sauce and mint jelly.
Yield: 6 servings

chicken spread

This is a basic spread. Try the variations for all seasons.

2 cups cold cooked chicken, cubed	**1 sweet pickle**
1 rib celery	**¼ to ⅓ cup mayonnaise**
1 small onion	**Salt and fresh ground pepper to taste**

Lock bowl in position. Insert **steel blade**. Add chicken. Clean celery and cut into 1'' pieces. Peel onion and cut into fourths. Cut pickle into several pieces. Add vegetables, pickle, and mayonnaise to chicken and process until mixture is blended. Season if necessary. Use as a sandwich spread.
Yield: About 2 cups

Summer-Curry: Add 1 teaspoon curry powder and ½ cup chopped coconut.

Spring-Peanut: Add ½ cup salted peanuts.

Winter-Tomato: Add 1 small tomato cut into eighths and a dash of rosemary. Use ¼ cup mayonnaise.

Fall-Thanksgiving: Add 1 teaspoon poultry seasoning to basic recipe.

corned beef crunch

Quickly made, this surprise could double for an hors d'oeuvre if cut into small squares.

8 to 10 sprigs parsley	**1 teaspoon prepared hot**
½ cup well-drained Chinese	**mustard**
vegetables	**6 slices wheat germ bread,**
2 cans (4½ ounces) corned beef	**buttered**
spread	

Lock bowl in position. Insert **steel blade**. Process parsley until chopped. Remove to a bowl. Add vegetables, corned beef spread, and mustard and process quickly to blend. Pile filling on buttered bread. Sprinkle with chopped parsley.
Yield: 6 open-faced sandwiches

cheese sandwich bake

A classic, this baked sandwich is good on the luncheon or supper menu with a mixed salad and a fruit dessert.

8 slices white bread	**3 eggs**
Softened butter	**2 cups milk**
2 cups cubed cooked ham	**¼ teaspoon salt**
2 tablespoons prepared mustard	**Fresh ground pepper to taste**
4 ounces sharp Cheddar cheese	

Cut crusts from bread. (Save and dry for bread crumbs.) Spread with softened butter and cut on diagonal to fit into a buttered 8'' x 8'' x 2'' baking dish. Put 4 slices on bottom of dish.

Lock bowl in position. Insert **steel blade**. Process 1 cup ham and 1 tablespoon prepared mustard at a time until finely chopped. Repeat. Spread on bread. Cut up cheese and process with **steel blade** until fine. Sprinkle on top of ham. Combine eggs with milk, salt, and pepper and process just to blend. Put remaining bread slices, butter side up, on ham and cheese. Gently pour egg mixture over bread. Refrigerate 1 hour. Bake at 325°F for 1 hour.
Yield: 4 to 6 servings

cheese buns

These toasted cheese buns make a nice accompaniment to a fruit salad or a cream soup.

½ pound processed American cheese	**1 egg**
1 small onion	**6 sandwich buns, split**
	Paprika

Let cheese stand at room temperature. Cut into 1'' cubes. Lock bowl in position. Insert **steel blade**. Peel onion and cut into small pieces. Combine cheese, onion, and egg in processor bowl and process until smooth. Spread on 12 halves of sandwich buns and sprinkle generously with paprika. Broil, 3'' from source of heat, until golden brown. Serve hot.
Yield: 12 halves

sandwich spreads

Carrot

2 medium carrots, peeled, cut in pieces	⅓ cup mayonnaise
4 sprigs fresh parsley	½ teaspoon salt
	1 teaspoon lemon juice

Peel carrots and cut into 1'' pieces. Lock bowl in position. Insert **steel blade**. Add carrots and parsley and process until finely chopped. Add mayonnaise, salt, and lemon juice and process 1 or 2 seconds just to blend.
Yield: 1⅓ cups

Cheese and Bologna

4 ounces sharp Cheddar cheese	1 teaspoon prepared mustard
4 ounces bologna	½ cup condensed tomato soup
1 small onion, if desired	

Cut cheese and bologna into cubes. Cut onion into fourths. Lock bowl in position. Insert **steel blade**. Add all ingredients to bowl and process until blended.
Yield: 1 cup

Mixed Cheese

4 ounces Roquefort cheese	¼ to ½ cup light cream
4 ounces American cheese	2 teaspoons paprika
1 tablespoon Worcestershire sauce	

Cut cheeses into cubes. Lock bowl in position. Insert **steel blade**. Combine all ingredients, using ¼ cup cream to start in bowl. Press until blended. If additional cream is needed, add through chute until desired consistency is reached.
Yield: 1½ cups

seaside special sandwich

Keep the ingredients on hand to make this hearty sandwich in a hurry.

2 hard-cooked eggs, peeled
1 can (7 ounces) tuna fish
1 tablespoon catsup
1 tablespoon lemon juice

3 tablespoons mayonnaise
8 slices buttered whole wheat bread
Lettuce

Lock bowl in position. Insert **steel blade**. Add eggs, tuna, catsup, lemon juice, and mayonnaise. Process just long enough to blend. Put generous spoonfull of filling on 4 slices of bread. Top with lettuce and remaining bread. Cut in half to serve.
Yield: 4 sandwiches

broiled shrimp salad sandwich

A hearty sandwich and a good lunch when served with tomato slices and a banana milk shake.

4 ounces sharp Cheddar cheese
¾ cup dairy sour cream
2 tablespoons seafood cocktail
    sauce

2 cans (4½ ounces) shrimp,
    well drained
3 hard-cooked eggs, peeled
6 slices toasted bread

Lock bowl in position. Insert **shredder disc**. Cut cheese to fit chute and grate cheese. Remove **shredder disc**, remove cheese to a bowl. Insert **steel blade**. Add sour cream, cocktail sauce, shrimp, and eggs cut in fourths. Process 1 or 2 seconds until mixture is blended.

    Place toast on broiler rack and pile filling on toast, spreading to cover piece completely. Sprinkle with grated cheese. Broil 3'' from source of heat until bubbly.
Yield: 6 servings

fresh vegetable salad sandwich

Frequently on menus in Ireland and England, these tempting sandwiches make a nice change—particularly during the season when garden-fresh vegetables are available. This is a basic recipe. Add or interchange vegetables to suit your taste.

1 carrot, peeled
1 rib celery
2 green onions
1 ripe tomato
1 cup fresh spinach

¼ head iceberg lettuce
½ teaspoon salt
Fresh ground pepper to taste
½ cup mayonnaise
8 slices whole wheat bread, buttered

Be sure all vegetables are cleaned and crisp. Lock bowl in position. Insert **steel blade**. Cut carrot, celery, and onion (both green and white part) into 1'' pieces. Process with **steel blade**, turning on and off to check size until medium-fine. Remove to a bowl. Remove stem end of tomato, cut into eighths and process with **steel blade** until medium-fine. Remove to bowl. Add spinach and lettuce to processor bowl and process with **steel blade** to chop coarsely. Add to bowl. Add mayonnaise and salt and pepper and mix lightly. Divide among 4 slices of bread and top with remaining bread.
Yield: 4 sandwiches

Pickles and Marmalades

It's a comforting thought to know that there are sparkling jars of marmalade, pickles, and chutney on the shelves, ready when needed. A big bonus for making your own is the knowledge of exactly what's in the jar. With the food processor as your helper, the work is literally cut in half. That should give you the inspiration to go to it.

Here are a few tips:

1. After jar is filled, run a spatula down side of jar to allow air bubbles to escape.
2. Seal jars. When getting ready to can pickles or whatever, put lids in a pan and pour boiling water over them to cover. The lids do not need to be boiled. After jars are filled, wipe rims with a clean, damp cloth. Put lid on jar with sealing composition next to jar rim. Screw band firmly tight, using full strength of hand.
3. Recent government tests show that it is safer if pickles and marmalades are processed in a boiling water bath. This means that the sealed jars should be put into a kettle of boiling water at least 1'' over top of jar. Bring water back to a boil and count time indicated from second boil. Remove from water at end of time.
4. Cool processed jars on rack. When cool, remove screw band. Wash jars. Label. Store in a cool, dark place.
5. Jelly test: Dip a metal spoon in the boiling jelly. As it nears the jellying point it will drop from the side of the spoon in two drops. When the drops run together and slide off in a sheet from the side of the spoon, the jelly is finished.

winter relish

Aptly named since all the ingredients are available in the winter, this relish is good with any meat or fish.

2 large sweet red peppers	2 teaspoons celery seed
2 large green peppers	4 cups sugar
2 medium heads cabbage	1 quart vinegar
1¼ pounds white onions	2 or 3 hot peppers, if desired
5 tablespoons salt	

Remove white ribs and seeds from peppers and cut into 1'' squares. Trim cabbage and cut into 1'' chunks. Peel onions and cut into quarters. Place bowl in position. Insert **steel blade** and chop peppers medium-fine. There should be 1 quart of peppers. As chopped, put into a large bowl. Chop cabbage. There should be 1 quart of cabbage. Add to peppers. Chop onions. There should be 2 cups of onions. Add to bowl. Mix vegetables with salt and let stand overnight. In the morning, drain off as much liquid as possible. Add celery seed, sugar, vinegar, and mix well to dissolve sugar. Pack into hot jars to within ½'' of top. Put a piece of hot pepper into each jar, if desired. Seal. Process 15 minutes in boiling water bath.
Yield: 5 to 6 pints

bread and butter pickles

Now you can make these long-time favorite sandwich pickles at home.

25 to 30 medium cucumbers, unwaxed	5 cups sugar
8 large white onions	2 tablespoons mustard seed
½ cup salt	1 teaspoon turmeric
5 cups cider vinegar	½ teaspoon whole cloves

Wash cucumbers well. Peel onions. Lock bowl in position. Insert **slicer disc**. Slice cucumbers and onions. Empty into large kettle as work bowl fills up. Stir salt into cucumbers and onions and let stand 3 hours. Drain.

Combine vinegar with remaining ingredients in a large kettle. Add cucumbers and onions and heat thoroughly, but do not boil. Pack into hot jars, leaving ½'' space at top. Wipe rims. Seal. Process 5 minutes in a boiling water bath.
Yield: 8 pints

pepper relish

This relish is great for hamburgers or hot dogs, and cold cuts, too.

6 to 8 medium green peppers
6 to 8 medium sweet red peppers
4 medium white onions

2 cups cider vinegar
1½ cups sugar
2 tablespoons salt

Wash peppers well. Remove white ribs and seeds and cut into 1'' squares. Peel and quarter onions. Lock bowl in position. Insert **steel blade**. Process to chop peppers and onions medium fine. Remove to a large kettle as chopped. When all chopping is done there should be 13 cups. Cover mixture with boiling water and let stand 10 minutes. Drain.

     Mix vinegar, sugar, and salt. Add pepper mixture. Bring to a boil and simmer 5 minutes, stirring constantly. Pack into hot jars, leaving ½'' space at top. Wipe rims. Seal. Process 5 minutes in a boiling water bath.
Yield: About 5 pints

california squash pickles

These zesty pickles will add interest to any meal.

2 pounds small yellow straight-
      neck squash
2 pounds zucchini squash
1 pound small onions
½ cup salt
1 quart wine vinegar

2 cups sugar
2 teaspoons celery seed
2 teaspoons turmeric
1 teaspoon dry mustard
2 teaspoons mustard seed

Wash squash well. Cut off and discard stem end. Lock bowl in position. Insert **slicer disc**. Cut squash to fit chute and process to slice. Remove to large bowl as work bowl gets filled. The squash should measure 4 quarts. Peel onions and feed through chute to slice. Add to squash. Onions should measure 3½ cups. Cover squash and onion with cold water and stir in salt. Let stand 1 hour and drain.

     Mix vinegar and sugar with seasonings. Bring to a boil and pour over squash and onion. Let stand 1 hour. Bring to a boil and cook 3 minutes. Pack into hot jars leaving ½'' space at top. Wipe rims. Seal. Process 5 minutes in a boiling water bath.
Yield: About 5 pints

chopped pickle relish

Try this with hamburgers.

8 large cucumbers, unwaxed
3 large green peppers
1 large sweet red pepper
1 large onion
1 tablespoon turmeric
½ cup salt

2 quarts cold water
2 tablespoons mustard seed
1 tablespoon celery seed
1½ cups firmly packed brown sugar
1 quart cider vinegar

Wash cucumbers well. Cut into 2'' pieces. Remove white ribs and seeds from peppers and cut into 1'' squares. Peel and quarter onion. Lock bowl in position. Insert **steel blade**. Chop cucumber, peppers, and onion, putting chopped food into a large bowl or pan as work bowl fills up.

When all vegetables are chopped, sprinkle turmeric over them and mix lightly with a fork. Combine salt with cold water and pour over vegetables. Let stand 4 hours. Drain. Cover vegetables with cold water and let stand 1 hour. Drain. Combine spices with sugar and vinegar in a large kettle and bring to a boil. Combine with vegetables and simmer for 15 minutes. Remove from heat and let stand 12 hours. Bring again to a boil and pack into hot jars leaving ½'' space at top. Seal. Process 5 minutes in boiling water bath.
Yield: About 6 pints

apple chutney

Chutney is particularly good with curry dishes. Now you can make your own.

12 apples
1 red pepper
2 green peppers
1 pint cider
½ cup orange marmalade
2 cups sugar

½ cup lemon juice
1 cup seedless raisins
1 tablespoon ground ginger
½ teaspoon Tabasco sauce
2 teaspoons salt

Peel apples, quarter, remove cores. Remove white ribs and seeds from peppers and cut into 1'' squares. Place bowl in position. Insert **steel blade**. Process apples to chop fine. As apples are chopped, put into large kettle. Process peppers. Add to kettle with remaining ingredients. Cook over low heat, stirring often, until mixture is thick. Ladle into hot jars. Seal. Process 5 minutes in a boiling water bath.
Yield: 3 pints

mincemeat

Imagine! Homemade mincemeat is now a breeze with the food processor.

2 pounds cooked lean beef
    or venison
1 pound beef suet
2 oranges
6 pounds apples
2 pounds currants
1 pound golden raisins
2 pounds seedless raisins

1 pound finely cut citron
3 pounds light brown sugar
2 teaspoons each allspice and nutmeg
3 teaspoons each cinnamon and salt
1 teaspoon cloves
¼ teaspoon ginger
8 cups apple juice

Lock bowl in position. Insert **steel blade**. Cut meat and suet into cubes and process medium fine 1 cup at a time. Cut 1 orange into eighths and process fine. Remove and discard peel from other orange, and process orange to medium fine.

Peel apples and remove core and cut into eighths. Process to medium coarse. As meat and fruit is being processed, put into a large kettle.

Add remaining ingredients and cook and stir over low heat, uncovered, 30 minutes, stirring often. Pack into hot jars, leaving 1'' at top. Wipe rims. Seal. Process in pressure canner at 10 pounds pressure for 20 minutes.
Yield: 10 quarts

spicy citrus tomato conserve

This spicy conserve is perfect with pork or chicken.

2 medium navel oranges
1 medium lemon
8 to 9 large firm ripe tomatoes
7 cups sugar

1 tablespoon whole cloves
2 sticks cinnamon
1 cup golden or dark seedless raisins

Wash fruit and cut thin slices off each end of oranges and lemon and discard. Cut fruit in half, lengthwise. With a shallow V-shaped cut, remove white center core and any seeds. Cut halves lengthwise again. Lock bowl in position and insert **slicer disc**. Fit quarters into chute and slice. Place sliced fruit in large kettle. Peel tomatoes, remove stem ends, and cut to fit chute. Feed into chute to slice. There should be 8 cups. Add to fruit in kettle along with sugar. Tie spices in a cheese-cloth bag and add to mixture. Bring to a boil, reduce heat, and gently boil for 1 hour, stirring frequently to avoid sticking. Remove spice bag and add raisins. Simmer slowly until mixture reaches jelly test or 222°F on candy thermometer. Ladle into hot jars. Seal. Process 10 minutes in boiling water bath.
Yield: 8 to 9 half-pint jars

chili sauce

An American favorite, this spicy sauce will be a happy companion to chicken, meat patties, pasta, or toasted cheese bread.

8 pounds ripe tomatoes
6 medium onions
4 medium green peppers
2 medium sweet red peppers
1 cup sugar
2 tablespoons salt

3 cups cider vinegar
1 tablespoon whole cloves
1 tablespoon whole allspice
1 tablespoon mustard seed
1 tablespoon Tabasco sauce

Peel tomatoes and cut into quarters. Peel onions and cut into quarters. Remove white ribs and seeds from peppers and cut into 1'' squares. Lock bowl in position. Insert **steel blade**. Process tomatoes, onions, and green peppers to chop fine. As work bowl fills, transfer food to a large kettle. Add sugar and salt. Tie spices in a cheesecloth bag and add to tomato mixture. Cook and stir over low heat, uncovered, about 2½ hours. Stir often toward last part of cooking to prevent sticking.
Remove spice bag. Add Tabasco. Ladle into hot pint or half-pint jars. Wipe rims. Seal. Process 5 minutes in boiling water bath.
Yield: 4 to 5 pints or 8 to 10 half pints

orange marmalade

This is a wonderful recipe for orange marmalade. You will be hooked once you make it!

10 medium navel oranges   **Water**
2 large lemons   **Sugar**

Wash oranges and lemons and cut off any spots and printing on peel. With a sharp paring knife, cut through peel into 6 sections and remove peel from oranges and lemons. Hold one end of section and remove white pith with a grapefruit spoon or a sharp paring knife. Peel off white membrane from oranges. Cut into quarters and remove seeds.

Lock bowl in position. Insert **slicer disc**. Fit orange and lemon peels into chute and process to slice. Put peel into a large bowl. Remove **slicer disc**. Insert **steel blade**. Add orange and lemon quarters to bowl and process to medium fine in 2 or 3 batches. Add to peel. Just cover with cold water and let stand overnight.

Next morning, pour contents of bowl into a large (3 quart) heavy kettle and cook until orange peel is tender, about 1 hour. Let stand 4 to 5 hours.

Weigh the orange mixture and add an equal amount of sugar. The mixture should weigh about 3½ pounds.

Cook until syrup gives the jelly test, or 222°F on a candy thermometer, stirring often to keep from burning. Ladle marmalade into hot jars. Fill to ½'' of top. Seal. Process 10 minutes in a boiling water bath.

Yield: 4 full pints

Index